ABOUT THE AUTHOR

Erich Fromm, German-born psychoanalyst, social philosopher, and author, was born in Frankfurt in 1900. He studied sociology and psychology at the universities of Heidelberg, Frankfurt, and Munich, and was trained in psychoanalysis at the Psychoanalytic Institute in Berlin. Since 1925 Fromm has devoted himself to consultant psychology and theoretical investigation.

Now an American citizen, Erich Fromm has lectured at Columbia University, Bennington College, the William Alanson White Institute of Psychiatry, the New School for Social Research, the National University of Mexico, and has been a Terry Lecturer at Yale University.

His books include: MAN FOR HIMSELF, PSYCHOANALYSIS AND RELIGION, THE FORGOTTEN LANGUAGE, THE SANE SOCIETY, THE ART OF LOVING, ZEN BUDDHISM AND PSYCHOANALYSIS (with D. T. Suzuki and R. de Martino), SIGMUND FREUD'S MISSION, MARX'S CONCEPT OF MAN, MAY MAN PREVAIL?, BEYOND THE CHAINS OF ILLUSION, THE DOGMA OF CHRIST AND OTHER ESSAYS, THE HEART OF MAN, and ESCAPE FROM FREEDOM.

ERICH FROMM

MAN
FOR
HIMSELF

An Inquiry

into the

Psychology of Ethics

FAWCETT PREMIER • NEW YORK

MAN FOR HIMSELF

THIS BOOK CONTAINS THE COMPLETE TEXT OF
THE ORIGINAL HARDCOVER EDITION.

Published by Fawcett Premier Books,
a unit of CBS Publications,
the Consumer Publishing Division of CBS Inc.,
by arrangement with Holt, Rinehart & Winston, Inc.

ISBN: 0-449-30819-7

Printed in the United States of America

First Fawcett Premier printing: September, 1965

27   26   25   24   23   22   21   20

FOREWORD

This book is in many respects a continuation of *Escape from Freedom*, in which I attempted to analyze modern man's escape from himself and from his freedom; in this book I discuss the problem of ethics, of norms and values leading to the realization of man's self and of his potentialities. It is unavoidable that certain ideas expressed in *Escape from Freedom* are repeated in this book, and although I have tried as much as possible to shorten discussions which are overlapping, I could not omit them entirely. In the chapter on Human Nature and Character, I discuss topics of characterology which were not taken up in the former book and make only brief reference to the problems discussed there. The reader who wishes to have a complete picture of my characterology must read both books, although this is not necessary for the understanding of the present volume.

It may be surprising to many readers to find a psychoanalyst dealing with problems of ethics and, particularly, taking the position that psychology must not only debunk false ethical judgments but can, beyond that, be the basis for building objective and valid norms of conduct. This position is in contrast to the trend prevailing in modern psychology which emphasizes "adjustment" rather than "goodness" and is on the side of ethical relativism. My experience as a practicing psychoanalyst has confirmed my conviction that problems of ethics can not be omitted from the study of personality, either theoretically or therapeutically. The value judgments we make determine our actions, and upon their validity rests our mental health and happiness. To consider evaluations only as so many rationalizations of unconscious, irrational desires—although they can be that too—narrows down and distorts our picture of the total personality. Neurosis itself is, in the last analysis, a symptom of moral failure (although "adjustment" is by no means a symptom of moral achievement). In many instances a neurotic symptom is the specific expression of moral conflict, and the success of the therapeutic effort depends on the understanding and solution of the person's moral problem.

The divorcement of psychology from ethics is of a comparatively recent date. The great humanistic ethical thinkers of the past, on whose works this book is based, were philosophers *and* psychologists; they believed that the understanding of man's nature and the understanding of values and norms for his life were interdependent. Freud and his school, on the other hand, though making an invaluable contribution to the progress of ethical thought by the debunking of irrational value judgments, took a relativistic position with regard to values, a position which had a negative effect not only upon the development of ethical theory but also upon the progress of psychology itself.

The most notable exception to this trend in psychoanalysis is C. G. Jung. He recognized that psychology and psychotherapy are bound up with the philosophical and moral problems of man. But while this recognition is exceedingly important in itself, Jung's philosophical orientation led only to a reaction against Freud and not to a philosophically oriented psychology going beyond Freud. To Jung "the unconscious" and the myth have become new sources of revelation, supposed to be superior to rational thought just because of their nonrational origin. It was the strength of the monotheistic religions of the West as well as of the great religions of India and China to be concerned with the truth and to claim that theirs was the true faith. While this conviction often caused fanatical intolerance against other religions, at the same time it implanted into adherents and opponents alike the respect for truth. In his eclectic admiration for any religion Jung has relinquished this search for the truth in his theory. Any system, if it is only nonrational, any myth or symbol, to him is of equal value. He is a relativist with regard to religion—the negative and not the opposite of rational relativism which he so ardently combats. This irrationalism, whether veiled in psychological, philosophical, racial, or political terms, is not

progress but reaction. The failure of eighteenth-
and nineteenth-century rationalism was not due to
its belief in reason but to the narrowness of its
concepts. Not less but more reason and an unabat-
ing search for the truth can correct errors of a
one-sided rationalism—not a pseudo-religious ob-
scurantism.

Psychology can not be divorced from philosophy
and ethics nor from sociology and economics. The
face that I have emphasized in this book the philosophical problems of psychology does not mean
that I have come to believe that the socio-economic factors are less important: this one-sided
emphasis is due entirely to considerations of
presentation, and I hope to publish another volume
on social psychology centered around the interaction of psychic and socio-economic factors.

It might seem that the psychoanalyst, who is in
the position of observing the tenacity and stub-
bornness of irrational strivings, would take a
pessimistic view with regard to man's ability to
govern himself and to free himself from the bondage of irrational passions. I must confess that during my analytic work I have become increasingly
impressed by the opposite phenomenon: by the
strength of the strivings for happiness and health,
which are part of the natural equipment of man.
"Curing" means removing the obstacles which
prevent them from becoming effective. Indeed,
there is less reason to be puzzled by the fact that
there are so many neurotic people than by the
phenomenon that most people are relatively
healthy in spite of the many adverse influences
they are exposed to.

One word of warning seems to be indicated.
Many people today expect that books on psychology will give them prescriptions on how to attain
"happiness" or "peace of mind." This book does
not contain any such advice. It is a theoretical
attempt to clarify the problem of ethics and psychology; its aim is to make the reader question
himself rather than to pacify him.

I cannot adequately express my indebtedness to
those friends, colleagues, and students whose stim-

ulation and suggestions helped me in writing the present volume. However, I wish to acknowledge specifically my gratitude to those who have contributed directly to the completion of this volume. Especially Mr. Patrick Mullahy's assistance has been invaluable; he and Dr. Alfred Seidemann have made a number of stimulating suggestions and criticisms in connection with the philosophical issues raised in the book. I am very much indebted to Professor David Riesman for many constructive suggestions and to Mr. Donald Slesinger who has improved the readability of the manuscript considerably. Most of all I am indebted to my wife, who helped with the revision of the manuscript and who made many significant suggestions with regard to the organization and the content of the book; particularly the concept of the positive and negative aspects of the nonproductive orientation owes much to her suggestions.

I wish to thank the editors of *Psychiatry* and of the *American Sociological Review* for permission to make use in the present volume of my articles "Selfishness and Self-Love," "Faith as a Character Trait," and "The Individual and Social Origins of Neurosis."

Furthermore, I wish to thank the following publishers for the privilege of using extensive passages from their publications: Board of Christian Education, the Westminster Press, Philadelphia, excerpts from *Institutes of the Christian Religion* by John Calvin, trans. by John Allen; Random House, New York, excerpts from the Modern Library Edition of *Eleven Plays of Henrik Ibsen;* Alfred A. Knopf, New York, excerpts from *The Trial* by F. Kafka, trans. by E. I. Muir; Charles Scribner's Sons, New York, excerpts from *Spinoza Selections,* edited by John Wild; the Oxford University Press, New York, excerpts from Aristotle's *Ethics,* trans. by W. D. Ross; Holt, Rinehart and Winston, Inc., New York, excerpts from *Principles of Psychology* by W. James; Appleton-Century-Crofts, New York, excerpts from *The Principles of Ethics,* Vol. I, by H. Spencer.

E. F.

CONTENTS

Be ye lamps unto yourselves.
Be your own reliance.
Hold to the truth within yourselves
as to the only lamp.

BUDDHA

True words always seem paradoxical but no other
form of teaching can take its place.

LAO-TSE

Who then are the true philosophers?
Those who are lovers of the vision of truth.

PLATO

My people are destroyed by the lack of knowledge;
because thou hast rejected knowledge
I will also reject thee.

HOSEA

If the way which, as I have shown, leads hither
seems very difficult, it can nevertheless be found.
It must indeed be difficult since it is so seldom
discovered, for if salvation lay ready to hand and
could be discovered without great labour, how
could it be possible that it should be neglected
almost by everybody? But all noble things are as
difficult as they are rare.

SPINOZA

CHAPTER I

THE PROBLEM

Surely, I said, knowledge is the food of the soul; and we must take care, my friend, that the Sophist does not deceive us when he praises what he sells, like the dealers wholesale or retail who sell the food of the body; for they praise indiscriminately all their goods, without knowing what are really beneficial or hurtful: neither do their customers know, with the exception of any trainer or physician who may happen to buy of them. In like manner those who carry about the wares of knowledge, and make the round of the cities, and sell or retail them to any customer who is in want of them, praise them all alike; though I should not wonder, O my friend, if many of them were really ignorant of their effect upon the soul; and their customers equally ignorant, unless he who buys of them happens to be a physician of the soul. If, therefore, you have understanding of what is good and evil you may safely buy knowledge of Protagoras or any one; but if not, then, O my friend, pause, and do not hazard your dearest interests at a game of chance. For there is far greater peril in buying knowledge than in buying meat and drink. . . .

—Plato, *Protagoras*

A spirit of pride and optimism has distinguished

Western culture in the last few centuries: pride in reason as man's instrument for his understanding and mastery of nature; optimism in the fulfillment of the fondest hopes of mankind, the achievement of the greatest happiness for the greatest number.

Man's pride has been justified. By virtue of his reason he has built a material world the reality of which surpasses even the dreams and visions of fairy tales and utopias. He harnesses physical energies which will enable the human race to secure the material conditions necessary for a dignified and productive existence, and although many of his goals have not yet been attained there is hardly any doubt that they are within reach and that the *problem of production*—which was the problem of the past—is, in principle, solved. Now, for the first time in his history, man can perceive that the idea of the unity of the human race and the conquest of nature for the sake of man is no longer a dream but a realistic possibility. Is he not justified in being proud and in having confidence in himself and in the future of mankind?

Yet modern man feels uneasy and more and more bewildered. He works and strives, but he is dimly aware of a sense of futility with regard to his activities. While his power over matter grows, he feels powerless in his individual life and in society. While creating new and better *means* for mastering nature, he has become enmeshed in a network of those means and has lost the vision of the end which alone gives them significance— *man himself*. While becoming the master of nature, he has become the slave of the machine which his own hands built. With all his knowledge about matter, he is ignorant with regard to the most important and fundamental questions of human existence: what man is, how he ought to live, and how the tremendous energies *within* man can be released and used productively.

The contemporary human crisis has led to a
retreat from the hopes and ideas of the Enlightenment under the auspices of which our political and
economic progress had begun. The very idea of
progress is called a childish illusion, and "realism,"
a new word for the utter lack of faith in man, is
preached instead. The idea of the dignity and
power of man, which gave man the strength and
courage for the tremendous accomplishments of
the last few centuries, is challenged by the suggestion that we have to revert to the acceptance of
man's ultimate powerlessness and insignificance.
This idea threatens to destroy the very roots from
which our culture grew.

The ideas of the Enlightenment taught man that
he could trust his own reason as a guide to establishing valid ethical norms and that he could rely
on himself, needing neither revelation nor the
authority of the church in order to know good and
evil. The motto of the Enlightenment, "dare to
know," implying "trust your knowledge," became
the incentive for the efforts and achievements of
modern man. The growing doubt of human autonomy and reason has created a state of moral
confusion where man is left without the guidance
of either revelation or reason. The result is the
acceptance of a relativistic position which proposes that value judgments and ethical norms are
exclusively matters of taste or arbitrary preference and that no objectively valid statement can
be made in this realm. But since man can not live
without values and norms, this relativism makes
him an easy prey for irrational value systems.
He reverts to a position which the Greek Enlightenment, Christianity, the Renaissance, and
the eighteenth-century Enlightenment had already
overcome. The demands of the State, the enthusiasm for magic qualities of powerful leaders,
powerful machines, and material success become
the sources for his norms and value judgments.

Are we to leave it at that? Are we to consent to the alternative between religion and relativism? Are we to accept the abdication of reason in matters of ethics? Are we to believe that the choices between freedom and slavery, between love and hate, between truth and falsehood, between integrity and opportunism, between life and death, are only the results of so many subjective preferences?

Indeed, there is another alternative. Valid ethical norms can be formed by man's reason and by it alone. Man is capable of discerning and making value judgments as valid as all other judgments derived from reason. The great tradition of humanistic ethical thought has laid the foundations for value systems based on man's autonomy and reason. These systems were built on the premise that in order to know what is good or bad for man one has to know the nature of man. They were, therefore, also fundamentally psychological inquiries.

If humanistic ethics is based on the knowledge of man's nature, modern psychology, particularly psychoanalysis, should have been one of the most potent stimuli for the development of humanistic ethics. But while psychoanalysis has tremendously increased our knowledge of man, it has not increased our knowledge of how man ought to live and what he ought to do. Its main function has been that of "debunking," of demonstrating that value judgments and ethical norms are the rationalized expressions of irrational—and often unconscious—desires and fears, and that they therefore have no claim to objective validity. While this debunking was exceedingly valuable in itself, it became increasingly sterile when it failed to go beyond mere criticism.

Psychoanalysis, in an attempt to establish psychology as a natural science, made the mistake of divorcing psychology from problems of philoso-

phy and ethics. It ignored the fact that human
personality can not be understood unless we look
at man in his totality, which includes his need to
find an answer to the question of the meaning of
his existence and to discover norms according to
which he ought to live. Freud's "homo psychologi-
cus" is just as much an unrealistic construction
as was the "homo economicus" of classical economics. It is impossible to understand man and
his emotional and mental disturbances without
understanding the nature of value and moral conflicts. The progress of psychology lies not in the
direction of divorcing an alleged "natural" from
an alleged "spiritual" realm and focusing attention
on the former, but in the return to the great tradition of humanistic ethics which looked at man in
his physico-spiritual totality, believing that man's
aim is *to be himself* and that the condition for
attaining this goal is that man be *for himself.*

I have written this book with the intention of
reaffirming the validity of humanistic ethics, to
show that our knowledge of human nature does
not lead to ethical relativism but, on the contrary,
to the conviction that the sources of norms for
ethical conduct are to be found in man's nature
itself; that moral norms are based upon man's
inherent qualities, and that their violation results
in mental and emotional disintegration. I shall
attempt to show that the character structure of
the mature and integrated personality, the productive character, constitutes the source and the
basis of "virtue" and that "vice," in the last analysis, is indifference to one's own self and self-
mutilation. Not self-renunciation nor selfishness
but self-love, not the negation of the individual
but the affirmation of his truly human self, are
the supreme values of humanistic ethics. If man
is to have confidence in values, he must know
himself and the capacity of his nature for goodness and productiveness.

CHAPTER II

HUMANISTIC ETHICS: THE APPLIED SCIENCE OF THE ART OF LIVING

Once Susia prayed to God: "Lord, I love you so much, but I do not fear you enough. Lord, I love you so much, but I do not fear you enough. Let me stand in awe of you as one of your angels, who are penetrated by your awe-filled name."

And God heard his prayer, and His name penetrated the hidden heart of Susia, as it comes to pass with the angels. But at that Susia crawled under the bed like a little dog, and animal fear shook him until he howled: "Lord, let me love you like Susia again."

And God heard him this time also.[1]

1. Humanistic vs. Authoritarian Ethics

If we do not abandon, as ethical relativism does, the search for objectively valid norms of conduct, what criteria for such norms can we find? The kind of criteria depends on the type of ethical system the norms of which we study. By necessity the criteria in authoritarian ethics are fundamentally different from those in humanistic ethics.

In authoritarian ethics an authority states what is good for man and lays down the laws and norms of conduct; in humanistic ethics man himself is

[1] In Time and Eternity, A Jewish Reader, edited by Nahum N. Glatzer (New York: Schocken Books, 1946).

18

both the norm giver and the subject of the norms, their formal source or regulative agency and their subject matter.]

The use of the term "authoritarian" makes it necessary to clarify the concept of authority. So much confusion exists with regard to this concept because it is widely believed that we are confronted with the alternative of having dictatorial, irrational authority or of having no authority at all. This alternative, however, is fallacious. The real problem is what *kind* of authority we are to have. When we speak of authority do we mean rational or irrational authority? *Rational authority* has its source in *competence*. The person whose authority is respected functions competently in the task with which he is entrusted by those who conferred it upon him. He need not intimidate them nor arouse their admiration by magic qualities; as long as and to the extent to which he is competently helping, instead of exploiting, his authority is based on rational grounds and does not call for irrational awe. Rational authority not only permits but requires constant scrutiny and criticism of those subjected to it; it is always temporary, its acceptance depending on its performance. The source of *irrational authority,* on the other hand, is always power over people. This power can be physical or mental, it can be realistic or only relative in terms of the anxiety and helplessness of the person submitting to this authority. Power on the one side, fear on the other, are always the buttresses on which irrational authority is built. Criticism of the authority is not only not required but forbidden. [Rational authority is based upon the equality of both authority and subject, which differ only with respect to the degree of knowledge or skill in a particular field. Irrational authority is by its very nature based upon inequality, implying difference in value.] In the use of the term "authoritarian ethics" refer-

ence is made to irrational authority, following
the current use of "authoritarian" as synonymous
with totalitarian and antidemocratic systems. The
reader will soon recognize that humanistic ethics
is not incompatible with rational authority.

Authoritarian ethics can be distinguished from
humanistic ethics by two criteria, one formal, the
other material. Formally, authoritarian ethics
denies man's capacity to know what is good or
bad; the norm giver is always an authority transcending the individual. Such a system is based
not on reason and knowledge but on awe of the
authority and on the subject's feeling of weakness
and dependence; the surrender of decision making
to the authority results from the latter's magic
power; its decisions can not and must not be
questioned. _Materially,_ or according to content,
authoritarian ethics answers the question of what
is good or bad primarily in terms of the interests
of the authority, not the interests of the subject;
it is exploitative, although the subject may derive
considerable benefits, psychic or material, from it.

Both the formal and the material aspects of
authoritarian ethics are apparent in the genesis
of ethical judgment in the child and of unreflective
value judgment in the average adult. The foundations of our ability to differentiate between good
and evil are laid in childhood; first with regard
to physiological functions and then with regard to
more complex matters of behavior. The child acquires a sense of distinguishing between good and
bad before he learns the difference by reasoning.
His value judgments are formed as a result of the
friendly or unfriendly reactions of the significant
people in his life. In view of his complete dependence on the care and love of the adult, it is not
surprising that an approving or disapproving
expression on the mother's face is sufficient to
"teach" the child the difference between good and
bad. In school and in society similar factors

operate. "Good" is that for which one is praised; "bad," that for which one is frowned upon or punished by social authorities or by the majority of one's fellow men. Indeed, the fear of disapproval and the need for approval seem to be the most powerful and almost exclusive motivation for ethical judgment. This intense emotional pressure prevents the child, and later the adult, from asking critically whether "good" in a judgment means good for him or for the authority. The alternatives in this respect become obvious if we consider value judgments with reference to things. If I say that one car is "better" than another, it is self-evident that one car is called "better" because it serves me better than another car; good or bad refers to the *usefulness* the thing has for *me*. If the owner of a dog considers the dog to be "good," he refers to certain qualities of the dog which to him are useful; as, for instance, that he fulfils the owner's need for a watch dog, a hunting dog, or an affectionate pet. A thing is called good if it is good for the person who uses it. With reference to man, the same criterion of value can be used. The employer considers an employee to be good if he is of advantage to him. The teacher may call a pupil good if he is obedient, does not cause trouble, and is a credit to him. In much the same way a child may be called good if he is docile and obedient. The "good" child may be frightened and insecure, wanting only to please his parents by submitting to their will, while the "bad" child may have a will of his own and genuine interests but ones which do not please the parents.

Obviously, the formal and material aspects of authoritarian ethics are inseparable. Unless the authority wanted to exploit the subject, it would not need to rule by virtue of awe and emotional submissiveness; it could encourage rational judgment and criticism—thus taking the risk of being found incompetent. But because its own interests are at stake the authority ordains *obedience to be the main virtue and disobedience to be the main sin.* The unforgivable sin in authoritarian ethics is rebellion, the questioning of the authority's right to establish norms and of its axiom that the norms established by the authority are in the best interest of the subjects. Even if a person sins, his acceptance of punishment and his feeling of guilt restore him to "goodness" because he thus expresses his acceptance of the authority's superiority.

The Old Testament, in its account of the beginnings of man's history, gives an illustration of authoritarian ethics. The sin of Adam and Eve is not explained in terms of the act itself; eating from the tree of knowledge of good and evil was not bad *per se;* in fact, both the Jewish and the Christian religions agree that the ability to differentiate between good and evil is a basic virtue. The sin was disobedience, the challenge to the authority of God, who was afraid that man, having already "become as one of Us, to know good and evil," could "put forth his hand and take also of the tree of life and live forever."

Humanistic ethics, in contrast to authoritarian ethics, may likewise be distinguished by formal and material criteria. *Formally,* it is based on the principle that only man himself can determine the criterion for virtue and sin, and not an authority transcending him. *Materially,* it is based on the principle that "good" is what is good for man and "evil" what is detrimental to man; *the sole criterion of ethical value being man's welfare.*

The difference between humanistic and authoritarian ethics is illustrated in the different meanings attached to the word "virtue." Aristotle uses "virtue" to mean "excellence"—excellence of the activity by which the potentialities peculiar to man are realized. "Virtue" is used, e.g., by Paracelsus as synonymous with the individual characteristics of each thing—that is, its peculiarity. A stone or a flower each has its virtue, its combination of specific qualities. Man's virtue, likewise, is that precise set of qualities which is characteristic of the human species, while each person's virtue is his unique individuality. He is "virtuous" if he unfolds his "virtue." In contrast, "virtue" in the modern sense is a concept of authoritarian ethics. To be virtuous signifies self-denial and obedience, suppression of individuality rather than its fullest realization.

Humanistic ethics is anthropocentric; not, of course, in the sense that man is the center of the universe but in the sense that his value judgments, like all other judgments and even perceptions, are rooted in the peculiarities of his existence and are meaningful only with reference to it; man, indeed, is the "measure of all things." The humanistic position is that there is nothing higher and nothing more dignified than human existence. Against this position it has been argued that it is in the very nature of ethical behavior to be related to something *transcending* man, and hence that a system which recognizes man and his interest alone cannot be truly moral, that its object would be merely the isolated, egotistical individual.

This argument, usually offered in order to disprove man's ability—and right—to postulate and to judge the norms valid for his life, is based on a fallacy, for the principle that good is what is *good for man* does not imply that man's nature is such that egotism or isolation are good for him. It does not mean that man's purpose can be fulfilled in a state of unrelatedness to the world outside him. In fact, as many advocates of humanistic ethics have suggested, it is one of the characteristics of human nature that man finds his fulfillment and happiness only in relatedness to and solidarity with his fellow men. However, to love one's neighbor is not a phenomenon *transcending* man; it is something inherent in and *radiating from* him. Love is not a higher power which descends upon man nor a duty which is imposed upon him; it is his own power by which he relates himself to the world and makes it truly his.

2. Subjectivistic vs. Objectivistic Ethics

If we accept the principle of humanistic ethics, what are we to answer those who deny man's capacity to arrive at normative principles which are *objectively* valid?

Indeed, one school of humanistic ethics accepts this challenge and agrees that value judgments have no objective validity and are nothing but arbitrary preferences or dislikes of an individual. From this point of view the statement, for instance, that "freedom is better than slavery" describes nothing but a difference in taste but is of no objective validity. Value in this sense is defined as "any desired good" and desire is the test of value, not value the test of desire. Such radical subjectivism is by its very nature incompatible with the idea that ethical norms should be universal and applicable to all men. If this subjectivism were the only kind of humanistic ethics then, indeed, we would be left with the choice between ethical authoritarianism and the abandonment of all claims for generally valid norms.

Ethical hedonism is the first concession made to the principle of objectivity: in assuming that pleasure is good for man and that pain is bad, it provides a principle according to which desires are rated: only those desires whose fulfillment causes pleasure are valuable; others are not. However, despite Herbert Spencer's argument that pleasure has an objective function in the process of biological evolution, pleasure can not be a criterion of value. For there are people who enjoy submission and not freedom, who derive pleasure from hate and not from love, from exploitation and not from productive work. This phenomenon of pleasure derived from what is objectively harmful is typical of the neurotic character and has been studied extensively by psychoanalysis. We shall come back to this problem in our discussion of character structure and in the chapter dealing with happiness and pleasure.

An important step in the direction of a more objective criterion of value was the modification of the hedonistic principle introduced by Epicurus, who attempted to solve the difficulty by differentiating between "higher" and "lower" orders of pleasure. But while the intrinsic difficulty of hedonism was thus recognized, the attempted solution remained abstract and dogmatic. Nevertheless, hedonism has one great merit: by making man's own experience of pleasure and happiness the sole criterion of value it shuts the door to all attempts to have an authority determine "what is best for man" without so much as giving man a chance to consider what he feels about that which is said to be best for him. It is not surprising, therefore, to find that hedonistic ethics in Greece, in Rome, and in modern European and American culture has been advocated by progressive thinkers who were genuinely and ardently concerned with the happiness of man.

But in spite of its merits hedonism could not establish the basis for objectively valid ethical judgments. Must we then give up objectivity if we choose humanism? Or is it possible to establish norms of conduct and value judgments which are objectively valid for all men and yet postulated by man himself and not by an authority transcending him? I believe, indeed, that this is possible and shall attempt now to demonstrate this possibility.

At the outset, let us not forget that "objectively valid" is not identical with "absolute." For instance, a statement of probability, of approximation, or any hypothesis can be valid and at the same time "relative" in the sense of having been established on limited evidence and being subject to future refinement if facts or procedures warrant it. The whole concept of relative vs. absolute is rooted in theological thinking in which a divine realm, as the "absolute," is separated from the imperfect realm of man. Except for this theological context the concept of absolute is meaningless and has as little place in ethics as in scientific thinking in general.

But even if we are agreed on this point, the main objection to the possibility of objectively valid statements in ethics remains to be answered: it is the objection that "facts" must be clearly distinguished from "values." Since Kant, it has been widely maintained that objectively valid statements can be made only about facts and not about values, and that one test of being scientific is the exclusion of value statements.

However, in the arts we are accustomed to lay down objectively valid norms, deduced from scientific principles which are themselves established by observation of fact and/or extensive mathematico-deductive procedures. The pure or "theoretical" sciences concern themselves with the discovery of facts and principles, although even in the physical and biological sciences a normative element enters which does not vitiate their objectivity. The applied sciences concern themselves primarily with practical norms according to which things ought to be *done*—where "ought" is determined by scientific knowledge of facts and principles. Arts are activities calling for specific knowledge and skill. While some of them demand only common-sense knowledge, others, such as the art of engineering or medicine, require an extensive body of theoretical knowledge. If I want to build a railroad track, for instance, I must build it according to certain principles of physics. *In all*

*arts a system of objectively valid norms consti-
tutes the theory of practice (applied science)
based on the theoretical science*. While there may
be different ways of achieving excellent results in
any art, norms are by no means arbitrary; their
violation is penalized by poor results or even by
complete failure to accomplish the desired end.

But not only medicine, engineering, and painting are arts; *living itself is an art* [2]—in fact, the
most important and at the same time the most
difficult and complex art to be practiced by man.
Its object is not this or that specialized performance, but the performance of living, the process
of developing into that which one is potentially. In
the art of living, *man is both the artist and the
object of his art;* he is the sculptor *and* the mar-
ble; the physician *and* the patient.

Humanistic ethics, for which "good" is synonymous with good for man and "bad" with bad for
man, proposes that in order to know *what* is good
for man we have to know his nature. *Humanistic
ethics is the applied science of the "art of living"
based upon the theoretical "science of man."* Here
as in other arts, the excellence of one's achievement ("virtus") is proportional to the knowledge
one has of the science of man and to one's skill and
practice. But one can deduce norms from theories
only on the premise that a certain activity is
chosen and a certain aim is desired. The premise
for medical science is that it is desirable to cure
disease and to prolong life; if this were not the
case, all the rules of medical science would be irrelevant. Every applied science is based on an
axiom which results from an act of choice:
namely, that the end of the activity is desirable.
There is, however, a difference between the axiom
underlying ethics and that of other arts. We can

---

[2] This use of "art," though, is in contrast to the terminology of Aristotle, who differentiates between "making" and
"doing."

imagine a hypothetical culture where people do not want paintings or bridges, but not one in which people do not want to live. The drive to live is inherent in every organism, and man can not help wanting to live regardless of what he would like to think about it.[3] The choice between life and death is more apparent than real; man's real choice is that between a good life and a bad life.

It is interesting at this point to ask why our time has lost the concept of *life as an art*. Modern man seems to believe that reading and writing are arts to be learned, that to become an architect, an engineer, or a skilled worker warrants considerable study, but that *living* is something so simple that no particular effort is required to learn how to do it. Just because everyone "lives" in some fashion, life is considered a matter in which everyone qualifies as an expert. But it is not because of the fact that man has mastered the art of living to such a degree that he has lost the sense of its difficulty. The prevailing lack of genuine joy and happiness in the process of living obviously excludes such an explanation. Modern society, in spite of all the emphasis it puts upon happiness, individuality, and self-interest, has taught man to feel that not his happiness (or if we were to use a theological term, his salvation) is the aim of life, but the fulfillment of his duty to work, or his success. Money, prestige and power have become his incentives and ends. He acts under the illusion that his actions benefit his self-interest, though he actually serves everything else *but* the interests of his real self. Everything is important to him except his life and the art of living. He is for everything except for himself.

If ethics constitutes the body of norms for achieving excellence in performing the art of liv-

---

[3] Suicide as a pathological phenomenon does not contradict this general principle.

ing, its most general principles must follow from the nature of life in general and of human existence in particular. In most general terms, the nature of all life is to preserve and affirm its own existence. All organisms have an inherent tendency to preserve their existence: it is from this fact that psychologists have postulated an "instinct" of self-preservation. The first "duty" of an organism is to be alive.

"To be alive" is a dynamic, not a static, concept. *Existence and the unfolding of the specific powers of an organism are one and the same.* All organisms have an inherent tendency to actualize their specific potentialities. *The aim of man's life,* therefore, is to be understood as *the unfolding of his powers according to the laws of his nature.*

Man, however, does not exist "in general." While sharing the core of human qualities with all members of his species, he is always an individual, a unique entity, different from everybody else. He differs by his particular blending of character, temperament, talents, dispositions, just as he differs at his fingertips. He can affirm his human potentialities only by realizing his individuality. The duty to be alive is the same as the duty to become oneself, to develop into the individual one potentially is.

To sum up, *good in humanistic ethics is the affirmation of life, the unfolding of man's powers. Virtue is responsibility toward his own existence.* Evil constitutes the crippling of man's powers; *vice is irresponsibility toward himself.*

These are the first principles of an objectivistic humanistic ethics. We cannot elucidate them here and shall return to the principles of humanistic ethics in Chapter IV. At this point, however, we must take up the question of whether a "science of man" is possible—as the theoretical foundation of an applied science of ethics.

3. The Science of Man[4]

The concept of a science of man rests upon the premise that its object, man, exists and that there is a human nature characteristic of the human species. On this issue the history of thought exhibits its special ironies and contradictions.

Authoritarian thinkers have conveniently assumed the existence of a human nature, which they believe was fixed and unchangeable. This assumption served to prove that their ethical systems and social institutions were necessary and unchangeable, being built upon the alleged nature of man. However, what they considered to be man's nature was a reflection of their norms—and interests—and not the result of objective inquiry. It was therefore understandable that progressives should welcome the findings of anthropology and psychology which, in contrast, seemed to establish the infinite malleability of human nature. For malleability meant that norms and institutions—the assumed cause of man's nature rather than the effect—could be malleable too. But in opposing the erroneous assumption that certain historical cultural patterns are the expression of a fixed and eternal human nature, the adherents of the theory of the infinite malleability of human nature arrived at an equally untenable position. First of all, the concept of the infinite malleability of human nature easily leads to conclusions which are as unsatisfactory as the concept of a fixed and unchangeable human nature. If man were infinitely malleable then, indeed, norms and institutions unfavorable to human wel-

---

[4] By "science of man" I refer to a broader concept than the conventional concept of anthropology. Linton has used science of man in a similarly comprehensive sense. Cf. *The Science of Man in the World Crisis*, ed. by Ralph Linton, Columbia University Press, New York, 1945.

fare would have a chance to mold man forever into their patterns without the possibility that intrinsic forces in man's nature would be mobilized and tend to change these patterns. Man would be only the puppet of social arrangements and not—as he has proved to be in history—an agent whose intrinsic properties react strenuously against the powerful pressure of unfavorable social and cultural patterns. In fact, if man were nothing but the reflex of culture patterns no social order could be criticized or judged from the standpoint of man's welfare since there would be no concept of "man."

As important as the political and moral repercussions of the malleability theory are its theoretical implications. If we assumed that there is no human nature (unless as defined in terms of basic physiological needs), the only possible psychology would be a radical behaviorism content with *describing* an infinite number of behavior patterns or one that *measures* quantitative aspects of human conduct. Psychology and anthropology could do nothing but describe the various ways in which social institutions and cultural patterns mold man and, since the special manifestations of man would be nothing but the stamp which social patterns have put on him, there could be only one science of man, comparative sociology. If, however, psychology and anthropology are to make valid propositions about the laws governing human behavior, they must start out with the premise that *something, say X, is reacting to environmental influences in ascertainable ways that follow from its properties*. Human nature is not fixed, and culture thus is not to be explained as the result of fixed human instincts; nor is culture a fixed factor to which human nature adapts itself passively and completely. It is true that man can adapt himself even to unsatisfactory conditions, but in this process of adaptation he develops definite mental and emotional reactions which follow from the specific properties of his own nature.

Man can adapt himself to slavery, but he reacts to it by lowering his intellectual and moral qualities; he can adapt himself to a culture permeated by mutual distrust and hostility, but he reacts to this adaptation by becoming weak and sterile. Man can adapt himself to cultural conditions which demand the repression of sexual strivings, but in achieving this adaptation he develops, as Freud has shown, neurotic symptoms. He can adapt himself to almost any culture pattern, but in so far as these are contradictory to his nature he develops mental and emotional disturbances which force him eventually to change these conditions since he can not change his nature.

Man is not a blank sheet of paper on which culture can write its text; he is an entity charged with energy and structured in specific ways, which, while adapting itself, reacts in specific and ascertainable ways to external conditions. If man had adapted himself to external conditions autoplastically, by changing his own nature, like an animal, and were fit to live under only one set of conditions to which he developed a special adaptation, he would have reached the blind alley of specialization which is the fate of every animal species, thus precluding history. If, on the other hand, man could adapt himself to all conditions without fighting those which are against his nature, he would have had no history either. Human evolution is rooted in man's adaptability and in certain indestructible qualities of his nature which compel him never to cease his search for conditions better adjusted to his intrinsic needs.

The subject of the science of man is human nature. But this science does not start out with a full and adequate picture of what human nature is; a satisfactory definition of its subject matter is its aim, not its premise. Its method is to observe the reactions of man to various individual and social conditions and from observation of these reactions to make inferences about man's nature. History and anthropology study the reactions of man to cultural and social conditions different from our own; social psychology studies his reactions to various social settings within our own culture. Child psychology studies the reactions of the growing child to various situations; psychopathology tries to arrive at conclusions about human nature by studying its distortions under pathogenic conditions. Human nature can never be observed as such, but only in its specific manifestations in specific situations. It is a theoretical construction which can be inferred from empirical study of the behavior of man. In this respect, the science of man in constructing a "model of human nature" is no different from other sciences which operate with concepts of entities based on, or controlled by, inferences from observed data and not directly observable themselves.

Despite the wealth of data offered by anthropology and psychology, we have only a tentative picture of human nature. For an empirical and objective statement of what constitutes "human nature," we can still learn from Shylock if we understand his words about Jews and Christians in the wider sense as representatives of all humanity.

"I am a Jew! Hath not a Jew eyes? hath not a Jew hands, organs, dimensions, senses, affections, passions? fed with the same food, hurt with the same weapons, subject to the same diseases, healed by the same means, warmed and cooled by the same winter and summer as a Christian is? If you prick us, do we not bleed? if you tickle us, do we not laugh? if you poison us, do we not die? and if you wrong us, shall we not revenge? If we are like you in the rest, we will resemble you in that."

4. The Tradition of Humanistic Ethics

In the tradition of humanistic ethics the view prevails that the knowledge of man is the basis of establishing norms and values. The treatises on ethics by Aristotle, Spinoza, and Dewey—the thinkers whose views we shall sketch in this chapter—are therefore at the same time treatises on psychology. I do not intend to review the history of humanistic ethics but only to give an illustration of its principle as expressed by some of its greatest representatives.

For *Aristotle,* ethics is built upon the science of man. Psychology investigates the nature of man and ethics therefore is applied psychology. Like the student of politics, the student of ethics "must know somehow the facts about the soul as the man who is to heal the eyes or the body as a whole must know about the eyes or body . . . but even among doctors the best educated spend much labour on acquiring knowledge of the body."[5] From the nature of man, Aristotle deduces the norm that "virtue" (excellence) is "activity," by which he means the exercise of the functions and capacities peculiar to man. Happiness, which is man's aim, is the result of "activity" and "use"; it is not a quiescent possession or state of mind. To explain his concept of activity Aristotle uses the Olympic Games as an analogy. "And, as in the Olympic Games," he says, "it is not the most beautiful and the strongest that are crowned, but those who compete (for it is some of these that are victorious), so those who act win, and rightly win, the

[5] *Ethica Nicomachea*, W. D. Ross, tr. (London, New York: Oxford University Press, 1925), 1102 a, 17–24.

noble and good things in life."[6] The free, rational, and active (contemplative) man is the good and accordingly the happy person. Here we have, then, objective value propositions which are man-centered or humanistic, and which are at the same time derived from the understanding of the nature and function of man.

Spinoza, like Aristotle, inquires into the distinctive function of man. He begins by considering the distinctive function and aim of *anything in nature* and answers that "each thing, as far as it is in itself, endeavours to persevere in its being."[7] Man, his function, and aim can be nothing else than that of any other thing: to preserve himself and to persevere in his existence. Spinoza arrives at a concept of virtue which is only the application of the general norm to the existence of man. "To act absolutely in conformity with virtue is, in us, nothing but acting, living and preserving our being (these three things have the same meaning) as *reason* directs, from the ground of seeking our own *profit*."[8]

Preserving one's being means to Spinoza *to become that which one potentially is.* This holds true for all things. "A horse," Spinoza says, "would be as much destroyed if it were changed into a man as if it were changed into an insect"; and we might add that, according to Spinoza, a man would be as much destroyed if he became an angel as if he became a horse. Virtue is the unfolding of the specific potentialities of every organism; for man it is the state in which he is most human. By *good*, consequently, Spinoza understands everything "which we are certain is a

---

[6] *Ibid.,* 1099 a, 3–5

[7] Benedictus de Spinoza, *Ethics,* W. Hale White, tr., revised by Amelia Hutcheson Sterling—Humphrey Milford (London: Oxford University Press, 1927), III, Prop. 6. (In Scribner's *Spinoza Selections.*)

[8] *Ibid.,* IV, Prop. 24.

means by which we may approach nearer and nearer to the *model of human nature He set before us*" (italics mine). By *evil* he understands "everything which we are certain hinders us from reaching that model."[9] Virtue is thus identical with the realization of man's nature; the science of man is consequently the theoretical science on which ethics is based.

While reason shows man what he ought to do in order to be truly himself and thus teaches him what is good, the way to achieve virtue is through the active use man makes of his powers. *Potency* thus is the same as virtue; *impotence*, the same as vice. Happiness is not an end in itself but is what accompanies the experience of increase in potency, while impotence is accompanied by depression; potency and impotence refer to all powers characteristic of man. Value judgments are applicable to man and his interests only. Such value judgments, however, are not mere statements of the likes and dislikes of individuals, for man's properties are intrinsic to the species and thus common to all men. The objective character of Spinoza's ethics is founded on the objective character of the model of human nature which, though allowing for many individual variations, is in its core the same for all men. Spinoza is radically opposed to authoritarian ethics. To him man is an end-in-himself and not a means for an authority transcending him. Value can be determined only in relation to his real interests, which are freedom and the productive use of his powers.[10]

[9] *Ibid.*, IV, Pref.

[10] *Marx* has expressed a view similar to Spinoza's: "To know what is useful for a dog," he says, "one must study dog-nature. This nature itself is not to be deduced from the principle of utility. Applying this to Man, he that would criticize all human acts, movements, relations, etc., by the principle of utility, must first deal with human nature in general, and then with human nature as modified in each historical epoch. Bentham makes short work of it. With

The most significant contemporary proponent of a scientific ethics is *John Dewey,* whose views are opposed both to authoritarianism and to relativism in ethics. As to the former, he states that the common feature of appeal to revelation, divinely ordained rulers, commands of the state, convention, tradition, and so on, "is that there is some voice so authoritative as to preclude the need of inquiry."[11] As to the latter, he holds that the fact that something is enjoyed is not in itself "a *judgment* of the value of what is enjoyed."[12] The enjoyment is a basic datum, but it has to be "verified by evidential facts."[13] Like Spinoza, he postulates that objectively valid value propositions can be arrived at by the power of human reason; for him, too, the aim of human life is the growth and development of man *in terms of his nature* and constitution. But his opposition to any fixed

---

the dryest naïveté, he takes the modern shopkeeper, especially the English shopkeeper, as the normal man." —Karl Marx, *Capital,* translated from the Third German Edition by Samuel Moore and Edward Aveling; edited by Frederick Engels; revised and amplified according to the Fourth German Edition by Ernest Untermann (New York: The Modern Library, Random House, Inc.), I, 688, footnote.

Spencer's view on ethics, in spite of significant philosophical differences, is also that "good" and "bad" follow the particular constitution of man and that the science of conduct is based on our knowledge of man. In a letter to J. S. Mill, Spencer says: "The view for which I contend is that Morality, properly so-called the science of right conduct, has for its object to determine *how* and *why* certain modes of conduct are detrimental and certain other modes beneficial. These good and bad results cannot be accidental but be *necessary consequences of the constitution of things.*"—Quoted by Spencer in *The Principles of Ethics,* Vol. I (New York: D. Appleton Co., 1902), p. 57.

[11] John Dewey and James H. Tufts, *Ethics* (New York: Henry Holt and Company, rev. ed., 1932), p. 364.

[12] John Dewey, *Problems of Men* (New York: Philosophical Library, 1946), p. 254.

[13] *Ibid.,* p. 260.

ends leads him to relinquish the important position
reached by Spinoza: that of a "model of human
nature" as a scientific concept. The main emphasis
in Dewey's position is on the relationship between
means and ends (or consequences) as the empirical
basis for the validity of norms. Valuation, according to him, takes place "only when there is something the matter; when there is some trouble to
be done away with, some need, lack, or privation
to be made good, some conflict of tendencies to be
resolved by means of changing existing conditions.
This fact in turn proves that there is present an
intellectual factor—a factor of inquiry—whenever there is valuation, for the end-in-view is
formed and projected as that which, if acted upon,
will supply the existing need or lack and resolve
the existing conflict."[14]

The end, to Dewey, "is merely a series of acts
viewed at a remote stage; and a means is merely
the series viewed at an earlier one. The distinction
of means and ends arises in surveying the *course*
of a proposed *line* of action, a connected series in
time. The 'end' is the last act thought of; the
means are the acts to be performed prior to it in
time. . . . Means and ends are two names for the
same reality. The terms denote not a division in
reality but a distinction in judgment."[15]

Dewey's emphasis on the interrelation between
means and ends is undoubtedly a significant point
in the development of a theory of rational ethics,
especially in warning us against theories which by
divorcing ends from means become useless. But
it does not seem to be true that "we do not *know*
what we are really after until a *course* of action

[14] John Dewey, "Theory of Valuation," in *International
Encyclopedia of Unified Science* (Chicago: The University
of Chicago Press, 1939), XI, No. 4, p. 34.

[15] John Dewey, *Human Nature and Conduct* (New York:
The Modern Library, Random House, 1930), pp. 34 f.

is mentally worked out."[16] Ends can be ascertained by the empirical analysis of the total phenomenon —of man—even if we do not yet know the means to achieve them. There are ends about which valid propositions can be made, although they lack at the moment, so to speak, hands and feet. The science of man can give us a picture of a "model of human nature" from which ends can be deduced before means are found to achieve them.[17]

5. Ethics and Psychoanalysis

From the foregoing it is, I think, apparent that the development of a humanistic-objectivistic ethics as an applied science depends on the development of psychology as a theoretical science. The progress from Aristotle's to Spinoza's ethics is largely due to the superiority of the latter's dynamic to the former's static psychology. Spinoza discovered unconscious motivation, the laws of association, the persistence of childhood experiences through life. His concept of desire is a dynamic concept, superior to Aristotle's "habit." But Spinoza's psychology, like all psychological thought up to the nineteenth century, tended to remain abstract and established no method for testing its theories by empirical investigation and exploration of new data concerning man.

Empirical inquiry is the key concept of Dewey's ethics and psychology. He recognizes unconscious motivation, and his concept of "habit" is different from the descriptive habit concept of traditional behaviorism. His statement[18] that modern clinical

---

[16] *Ibid.*, p. 36.

[17] Utopias are visions of ends before the realization of means, yet they are not meaningless; on the contrary, some have contributed greatly to the progress of thought, not to speak of what they have meant to uphold faith in the future of man.

[18] Dewey, *Human Nature and Conduct*, p. 86.

psychology "exhibits a sense for reality in its insistence upon the profound importance of unconscious forces in determining not only overt conduct but desire, judgment, belief, idealization" shows the importance he attributes to unconscious factors even though he did not exhaust all possibilities of this new method in his theory of ethics.

Few attempts have been made either from the philosophical or from the psychological side to apply the findings of psychoanalysis to the development of ethical theory,[19] a fact that is all the more surprising since psychoanalytic theory has made contributions which are particularly relevant to the theory of ethics.

The most important contribution, perhaps, is the fact that psychoanalytic theory is the first modern psychological system the subject matter of which is not isolated aspects of man but his total personality. Instead of the method of conventional psychology, which had to restrict itself to the study of such phenomena as could be isolated sufficiently to be observed in an experiment, *Freud* discovered a new method which enabled him to study the total personality and to understand what makes man act as he does. This method, the analysis of free associations, dreams, errors, transference, is an approach by which

---

[19] A brief but significant contribution to the problem of values from the psychoanalytic viewpoint is *Patrick Mullahy's* article, "Values, Scientific Method and Psychoanalysis," *Psychiatry*, May, 1943. During the revision of the manuscript of this book, J. C. Flugel's *Man, Morals and Society* was published (New York: International Universities Press, 1945), which is the first systematic and serious attempt of a psychoanalyst to apply psychoanalytic findings to ethical theory. A very valuable statement of the problems and a profound criticism—although going far beyond criticism—of the psychoanalytic view on ethics is to be found in Mortimer J. Adler's *What Man Has Made of Man* (New York: Longmans, Green & Co., 1937).

hitherto "private" data, open only to self-knowledge and introspection, are made "public" and demonstrable in the communication between subject and analyst. The psychoanalytic method has thus gained access to phenomena which do not otherwise lend themselves to observation. At the same time it uncovered many emotional experiences which could not be recognized. even by introspection because they were repressed, divorced from consciousness.[20]

At the beginning of his studies Freud was mainly interested in neurotic symptoms. But the more psychoanalysis advanced, the more apparent it became that a neurotic symptom can be understood only by understanding the character structure in which it is embedded. The neurotic *character*, rather than the symptom, became the main subject matter of psychoanalytic theory and therapy. In his pursuit of the study of the neurotic character Freud laid new foundations for a science of character (characterology), which in recent centuries had been neglected by psychology and left to the novelists and playwrights.

Psychoanalytic characterology, though still in its infancy, is indispensable to the development of ethical theory. All the virtues and vices with which traditional ethics deals must remain ambiguous because they often signify by the same word different and partly contradictory human attitudes; they lose their ambiguity only if they are understood in connection with the character structure of the person of whom a virtue or vice is predicated. A virtue isolated from the context of character may turn out to be nothing valuable (as, for instance, humility caused by fear or compensating for suppressed arrogance); or a vice

[20] Cf. Dewey, *Problems of Men*, pp. 250–272, and Philip B. Rice, "Objectivity of Value Judgment and Types of Value Judgment," *Journal of Philosophy*, XV (1934), 5–14, 533–543.

will be viewed in a different light if understood in the context of the whole character (as, for instance, arrogance as an expression of insecurity and self-depreciation). This consideration is exceedingly relevant to ethics; it is insufficient and misleading to deal with isolated virtues and vices as separate traits. The subject matter of ethics is *character*, and only in reference to the character structure as a whole can value statements be made about single traits or actions. *The virtuous or the vicious character, rather than single virtues or vices, is the true subject matter of ethical inquiry.*

No less significant for ethics is the psychoanalytic concept of *unconscious* motivation. While this concept, in a general form, dates back to Leibniz and Spinoza, Freud was the first to study unconscious strivings empirically and in great detail, and thus to lay the foundations of a theory of human motivations. The evolution of ethical thought is characterized by the fact that value judgments concerning human conduct were made in reference to the motivations underlying the act rather than to the act itself. Hence the understanding of unconscious motivation opens up a new dimension for ethical inquiry. Not only "what is lowest," as Freud remarked, "but also what is highest in the Ego can be unconscious"[21] and be the strongest motive for action which ethical inquiry can not afford to ignore.

In spite of the great possibilities which psychoanalysis provides for the scientific study of values, Freud and his school have not made the most productive use of their method for the inquiry into ethical problems; in fact, they did a great deal to confuse ethical issues. The confusion springs from Freud's relativistic position, which assumes

[21] S. Freud, *The Ego and the Id*, Joan Riviere & V. Woolf tr. (London: Hogarth Press and the Institute of Psychoanalysis, 1935), p. 133.

that psychology can help us to understand the *motivation* of value judgments but can not help in establishing the *validity* of the value judgments themselves.

Freud's relativism is indicated most distinctly in his theory of the Super-Ego (conscience). According to this theory, anything can become the content of conscience if only it happens to be part of the system of commands and prohibitions embodied in the father's Super-Ego and the cultural tradition. *Conscience in this view is nothing but internalized authority.* Freud's analysis of the Super-Ego is the analysis of the "authoritarian conscience" only.[22]

A good illustration of this relativistic view is the article by T. Schroeder entitled "Attitude of One Amoral Psychologist."[23] The author comes to the conclusion that "every moral valuation is the product of emotional morbidity—intense conflicting impulses—derived from past emotional experiences," and that the amoral psychiatrist "will replace moral standards, values and judgments by the psychiatric and psycho-evolutionary classification of the moralist impulses and intellectual methods." The author then proceeds to confuse the issue by stating that "the amoral evolutionary psychologists have no *absolute or eternal rules* of right or wrong about anything," thus making it appear as if science did make "absolute and eternal" statements.

Slightly different from Freud's Super-Ego theory is his view that morality is essentially a reaction formation against the evil inherent in man. He proposes that the child's sexual strivings are directed toward the parent of the opposite sex; that in consequence he hates the parental rival

---

[22] A more detailed discussion of conscience is to be found in Chapter IV.

[23] *The Psychoanalytic Review*, XXXI, No. 3 (July, 1944), 329–335.

of the same sex, and that hostility, fear, guilt thus *necessarily* spring from this early situation (Oedipus complex). This theory is the secularized version of the concept of "original sin." Since these incestuous and murderous impulses are integral parts of man's nature, Freud reasoned, man had to develop ethical norms in order to make social life possible. Primitively, in a system of tabus, and later on, in less primitive systems of ethics, man established norms of social behavior in order to protect the individual and the group from the dangers of these impulses.

However, Freud's position is by no means consistently relativistic. He displays a passionate faith in truth as the aim toward which man must strive, and he believes in man's capacity thus to strive since he is by nature endowed with reason. This anti-relativistic attitude is clearly expressed in his discussions of "a philosophy of life."[24] He opposes the theory that truth is "only the product of our own needs and desires, as they are formulated under varying external conditions"; in his opinion such an "anarchistic" theory "breaks down the moment it comes in contact with practical life." His belief in the power of reason and its capacity to unify mankind and to free man from the shackles of superstition has the pathos characteristic of the Enlightenment philosophy. This faith in truth underlies his concept of psychoanalytic cure. Psychoanalysis is the attempt to uncover the truth about oneself. In this respect Freud continues the tradition of thought which, since Buddha and Socrates, believes in truth as the power that makes man virtuous and free, or —in Freud's terminology—"healthy." The aim of analytic cure is to replace the irrational (the id)

[24] S. Freud, *New Introductory Lectures on Psychoanalysis*, W. J. H. Sprott, tr. (New York: W. W. Norton & Company, 1937), pp. 240–241.

by reason (the ego). The analytic situation may be defined from this standpoint as one where two people—the analyst and the patient—devote themselves to the search for truth. The aim of the cure is the restoring of health, and the remedies are truth and reason. To have postulated a situation based upon radical honesty within a culture in which such frankness is rare is perhaps the greatest expression of Freud's genius.

In his characterology, too, Freud presents a nonrelativistic position, although only by implication. He assumes that the libido development continues from the oral through the anal and to the genital stage, and that in the healthy person the genital orientation becomes predominant. Although Freud did not refer to ethical values explicitly, there is an implicit connection: the pregenital orientations, characteristic of the dependent, greedy, and stingy attitudes, are ethically inferior to the genital, that is, productive, mature character. Freud's characterology thus implies that virtue is the natural aim of man's development. This development can be blocked by specific and mostly extraneous circumstances and it can thus result in the formation of the neurotic character. Normal growth, however, will produce the mature, independent, productive character, capable of loving and of working; in the last analysis, then, to Freud health and virtue are the same.

But this connection between character and ethics is not made explicit. It had to remain confused, partly because of the contradiction between Freud's relativism and the implicit recognition of humanistic ethical values and partly because, while concerned mainly with the neurotic character, Freud devoted little attention to the analysis and description of the genital and mature character.

The following chapter, after reviewing the

"human situation" and its significance for character development, leads up to a detailed analysis of the equivalent of the genital character, the "productive orientation."

CHAPTER III

HUMAN NATURE AND CHARACTER

That I am a man,
this I share with other men.
That I see and hear and
that I eat and drink
is what all animals do likewise.
But that I am I is only mine
and belongs to me
and to nobody else;
to no other man
not to an angel nor to God—
except inasmuch
as I am one with Him.

—Master Eckhart,
Fragments

1. *The Human Situation*

One individual represents the human race. He is one specific example of the human species. He is "he" and he is "all"; he is an individual with his peculiarities and in this sense unique, and at the same time he is representative of all characteristics of the human race. His individual personality is determined by the peculiarities of human existence common to all men. Hence the discussion of the human situation must precede that of personality.

A. MAN'S BIOLOGICAL WEAKNESS

The first element which differentiates human from animal existence is a negative one: the relative absence in man of instinctive regulation in the process of adaptation to the surrounding world. The mode of adaptation of the animal to its world remains the same throughout; if its instinctual equipment is no longer fit to cope successfully with a changing environment the species will die out. The animal can adapt itself to changing conditions by changing itself—autoplastically; not by changing its environment—alloplastically. In this fashion it lives harmoniously, not in the sense of absence of struggle but in the sense that its inherited equipment makes it a fixed and unchanging part of its world; it either fits in or dies out.

The less complete and fixed the instinctual equipment of animals, the more developed is the brain and therefore the ability to learn. The emergence of man can be defined as occurring at the point in the process of evolution where instinctive adaptation has reached its minimum. But he emerges with new qualities which differentiate him from the animal: his awareness of himself as a separate entity, his ability to remember the past, to visualize the future, and to denote objects and acts by symbols; his reason to conceive and understand the world; and his imagination through which he reaches far beyond the range of his senses. Man is the most helpless of all animals, but this very biological weakness is the basis for his strength, the prime cause for the development of his specifically human qualities.

B. THE EXISTENTIAL AND THE HISTORICAL DICHOTOMIES IN MAN

Self-awareness, reason, and imagination have disrupted the "harmony" which characterizes animal existence. Their emergence has made man into an anomaly, into the freak of the universe. He is part of nature, subject to her physical laws and unable to change them, yet he transcends the rest of nature. He is set apart while being a part; he is homeless, yet chained to the home he shares with all creatures. Cast into this world at an accidental place and time, he is forced out of it, again accidentally. Being aware of himself, he realizes his powerlessness and the limitations of his existence. He visualizes his own end: death. Never is he free from the dichotomy of his existence: he cannot rid himself of his mind, even if he should want to; he cannot rid himself of his body as long as he is alive—and his body makes him want to be alive.

Reason, man's blessing, is also his curse; it forces him to cope everlastingly with the task of solving an insoluble dichotomy. Human existence is different in this respect from that of all other organisms; it is in a state of constant and unavoidable disequilibrium. Man's life cannot "be lived" by repeating the pattern of his species; *he* must live. Man is the only animal that can be *bored*, that can be *discontented*, that can feel evicted from paradise. Man is the only animal for whom his own existence is a problem which he has to solve and from which he cannot escape. He cannot go back to the prehuman state of harmony with nature; he must proceed to develop his reason until he becomes the master of nature, and of himself.

The emergence of reason has created a dichotomy within man which forces him to strive everlastingly for new solutions. The dynamism of his history is intrinsic to the existence of reason which causes him to develop and, through it, to create a world of his own in which he can feel at home with himself and his fellow men. Every stage he reaches leaves him discontented and perplexed, and this very perplexity urges him to move toward new solutions. There is no innate "drive for progress" in man; it is the contradiction in his existence that makes him proceed on the way he set out. Having lost paradise, the unity with nature, he has become the eternal wanderer (Odysseus, Oedipus, Abraham, Faust); he is impelled to go forward and with everlasting effort to make the unknown known by filling in with answers the blank spaces of his knowledge. He must give account to himself of himself, and of the meaning of his existence. He is driven to overcome this inner split, tormented by a craving for "absoluteness," for another kind of harmony which can lift the curse by which he was separated from nature, from his fellow men, and from himself.

This split in man's nature leads to dichotomies which I call existential[1] because they are rooted in the very existence of man; they are contradictions which man cannot annul but to which he can react in various ways, relative to his character and his culture.

The most fundamental existential dichotomy is that between life and death. The fact that we have to die is unalterable for man. Man is aware of this fact, and this very awareness profoundly influences his life. But death remains the very opposite of life and is extraneous to, and incompatible with, the experience of living. All knowledge *about* death does not alter the fact that death is not a meaningful part of life and that there is nothing for us to do but to accept the fact of death; hence, as far as our life is concerned,

---

[1] I have used this term without reference to the terminology of existentialism. During the revision of the manuscript I became acquainted with Jean-Paul Sartre's *Flies* and his *Is Existentialism a Humanism?* I do not feel that any changes or additions are warranted. Although there are certain points in common, I cannot judge the degree of agreement since I have had as yet no access to Sartre's main philosophical opus.

defeat. "All that man has will he give for his life" and "the wise man," as Spinoza says, "thinks not of death but of life." Man has tried to negate this dichotomy by ideologies, e.g., the Christian concept of immortality, which, by postulating an immortal soul, denies the tragic fact that man's life ends with death.

That man is mortal results in another dichotomy: while every human being is the bearer of all human potentialities, the short span of his life does not permit their full realization under even the most favorable circumstances. Only if the life span of the individual were identical with that of mankind could he participate in the human development which occurs in the historical process. Man's life, beginning and ending at one accidental point in the evolutionary process of the race, conflicts tragically with the individual's claim for the realization of all of his potentialities. Of this contradiction between what he *could* realize and what he actually does realize he has, at least, a dim perception. Here, too, ideologies tend to reconcile or deny the contradiction by assuming that the fulfillment of life takes place after death, or that one's own historical period is the final and crowning achievement of mankind. Still another maintains that the meaning of life is not to be found in its fullest unfolding but in social service and social duties; that the development, freedom, and happiness of the individual is subordinate to or even irrelevant in comparison with the welfare of the state, the community, or whatever else may symbolize eternal power, transcending the individual.

Man is alone and he is related at the same time. He is alone inasmuch as he is a unique entity, not identical with anyone else, and aware of his self as a separate entity. He must be alone when he has to judge or to make decisions solely by the power of his reason. And yet he cannot bear to be alone, to be unrelated to his fellow men. His happiness depends on the solidarity he feels with his fellow men, with past and future generations.

Radically different from existential dichotomies are the many historical contradictions in individual and social life which are not a necessary part of human existence but are man made and soluble, soluble either at the time they occur or at a later period of human history. The contemporary contradiction between an abundance of technical means for material satisfaction and the incapacity to use them exclusively for peace and the welfare of the people is soluble; it is not a necessary contradiction but one due to man's lack of courage and wisdom. The institution of slavery in ancient Greece may be an example of a relatively insoluble contradiction, the solution of which could be achieved only at a later period of history when the material basis for the equality of man was established.

The distinction between existential and historical dichotomies is significant because their confusion has far-reaching implications. Those who were interested in upholding the historical contradictions were eager to prove that they were existential dichotomies and thus unalterable. They tried to convince man that "what must not be cannot be" and that he had to resign himself to the acceptance of his tragic fate. But this attempt to confuse these two types of contradictions was not sufficient to keep man from trying to solve them. It is one of the peculiar qualities of the human mind that, when confronted with a contradiction, it cannot remain passive. It is set in motion with the aim of resolving the contradiction. All human progress is due to this fact. If man is to be prevented from reacting to his awareness of contradictions by action, the very existence of these contradictions must be denied. To harmonize, and thus negate, contradictions is the function of rationalizations in individual life and of ideologies (socially patterned rationalizations) in social life. However, if man's mind could be satisfied only by rational answers, by the truth, these ideologies would remain ineffective. But it is also one of his peculiarities to accept as truth the thoughts shared by most of the members of his culture or postulated by powerful authorities. If the harmonizing ideologies are supported by consensus or authority, man's mind is appeased although he himself is not entirely set at rest.

Man can react to historical contradictions by annulling them through his own action; but he cannot annul existential dichotomies, although he can react to them in different ways. He can appease his mind by soothing and harmonizing ideologies. He can try to escape from his inner restlessness by ceaseless activity in pleasure or business. He can try to abrogate his freedom and to turn himself into an instrument of powers outside himself, submerging his self in them. But he remains dissatisfied, anxious, and restless. There is only one solution to his problem: to face the truth, to acknowledge his fundamental aloneness and solitude in a universe indifferent to his fate, to recognize that there is no power transcending him which can solve his problem for him. Man must accept the responsibility for himself and the fact that only by using his own powers can he give meaning to his life. But meaning does not imply certainty; indeed, the quest for certainty blocks the search for meaning. Uncertainty is the very condition to impel man to unfold his powers. If he faces the truth without panic he will recognize that *there is no meaning to life except the meaning man gives his life by the unfolding of his powers, by living productively;* and that only constant vigilance, activity, and effort can keep us from failing in the one task that matters—the full development of our powers within the limitations set by the laws of our existence. Man will never cease to be perplexed, to wonder, and to raise new questions. Only if he recognizes the human situation, the dichotomies inherent in his existence and his capacity to unfold his powers, will he be able to succeed in his task: to be himself and for himself and to achieve happiness by the full realization of those faculties which are peculiarly his—of reason, love, and productive work.

After having discussed the existential dichotomies inherent in man's existence we can return to the statement made in the beginning of this chapter that the discussion of the human situation must precede that of personality. The more precise meaning of this statement can be made apparent by stating that psychology must be based on an anthropologico-philosophical concept of human existence.

The most striking feature in human behavior is the tremendous intensity of passions and strivings which man displays. Freud more than anyone else recognized this fact and attempted to explain it in terms of the mechanistic-naturalistic thinking of his time. He assumed that those passions which were not the obvious expressions of the instinct of self-preservation and of the sexual instinct (or as he formulated it later of Eros and the Death instinct) were nevertheless only more indirect and complicated manifestations of these instinctual-biological drives. But brilliant as his assumptions were they are not convincing in their denial of the fact that a large part of man's passionate strivings cannot be explained by the force of his instincts. Even if man's hunger and thirst and his sexual strivings are completely satisfied "he" is not satisfied. In contrast to the animal his most compelling problems are not solved then, they only begin. He strives for power, or for love, or for destruction, he risks his life for religious, for political, for humanistic ideals, and these strivings are what constitutes and characterizes the peculiarity of human life. Indeed, "man does not live by bread alone."

In contrast to Freud's mechanistic-naturalistic explanation this statement has been interpreted to mean that man has an intrinsic religious need which cannot be explained by his natural existence but must be explained by something transcending him and which is derived from supernatural powers. However, the latter assumption is unnecessary since the phenomenon can be explained by the full understanding of the human situation.

The disharmony of man's existence generates needs which far transcend those of his animal origin. These needs result in an imperative drive to restore a unity and equilibrium between himself and the rest of nature. He makes the attempt to restore this unity and equilibrium in the first place in thought by constructing an all-inclusive mental picture of the world which serves as a frame of reference from which he can derive an answer to the question of where he stands and what he ought to do. But such thought-systems are not sufficient. If man were only a disembodied intellect his aim would be achieved by a comprehensive thought-system. But since he is an entity endowed with a body as well as a mind he has to react to the dichotomy of his existence not only in thinking but also in the process of living, in his feelings and actions. He has to strive for the experience of unity and oneness in all spheres of his being in order to find a new equilibrium. Hence any satisfying system of orientation implies not only intellectual elements but elements of feeling and sense to be realized in action in all fields of human endeavor. Devotion to an aim, or an idea, or a power transcending man such as God, is an expression of this need for completeness in the process of living.

The answers given to man's need for an orientation and for devotion differ widely both in content and in form. There are primitive systems such as animism and totemism in which natural objects or ancestors represent answers to man's quest for meaning. There are non-theistic systems like Buddhism, which are usually called religious although in their original form there is no concept of God. There are philosophical systems, like Stoicism, and there are the monotheistic religious systems which give an answer to man's quest for meaning in reference to the concept of God. In discussing these various systems, we are hampered by a terminological difficulty. We could call them all religious systems were it not for the fact that for historical reasons the word "religious" is identified with a theistic system, a system centered around God, and we simply do not have a word in our language to denote that which is common to both theistic and non-theistic systems—that is, to all systems of thought which try to give an answer to the human quest for meaning and to man's attempt to make sense of his own existence. For lack of a better word I therefore call such systems "frames of orientation and devotion."

The point, however, I wish to emphasize is that there are many other strivings which are looked upon as entirely secular which are nevertheless rooted in the same need from which religious and philosophical systems spring. Let us consider what we observe in our time: We see in our own culture millions of people devoted to the attainment of success and prestige. We have seen and still see in other cultures fanatical devotion of adherents to dictatorial systems of conquest and domination. We are amazed at the intensity of those passions which is often stronger than even the drive for self-preservation. We are easily deceived by the *secular* contents of these aims and explain them as outcomes of sexual or other quasi-biological strivings. But is it not apparent that the intensity and fanaticism with which these secular aims are pursued is the same as we find in religions; that all these secular systems of orientation and devotion differ in content but not in the basic need to which they attempt to offer answers? In our culture the picture is so particularly deceptive because most people "believe" in monotheism while their actual devotion belongs to systems which are, indeed, much closer to totemism and worship of idols than to any form of Christianity.

But we must go one step further. The understanding of the "religious" nature of these culturally patterned secular strivings is the key to the understanding of neuroses and irrational strivings. We have to consider the latter as answers— individual answers—to man's quest for orientation and devotion. A person whose experience is determined by "his fixation to his family," who is incapable of acting independently is in fact a worshiper of a primitive ancestor cult, and the only difference between him and millions of ancestor worshipers is that his system is private and not culturally patterned. Freud recognized the connection between religion and neurosis and explained religion as a form of neurosis, while we arrive at the conclusion that a neurosis is to be explained as a particular form of religion differing mainly by its individual, non-patterned characteristics. The conclusion to which we are led with regard to the general problem of human motivation is that while the need for a system of orientation and devotion is common to all men, the particular *contents* of the systems which satisfy this need differ. These differences are differences in value; the mature, productive, rational person will choose a system which permits him to be mature, productive and rational. The person who has been blocked in his development must revert to primitive and irrational systems which in turn prolong and increase his dependence and irrationality. He will remain on the level which mankind in its best representatives has already overcome thousands of years ago.

Because the need for a system of orientation and devotion is an intrinsic part of human existence we can understand the intensity of this need. Indeed, there is no other more powerful source of energy in man. Man is not free to choose between having or not having "ideals," but he is free to choose between different kinds of ideals, between being devoted to the worship of power and destruction and being devoted to reason and love. All men are "idealists" and are striving for something beyond the attainment of physical satisfaction. They differ in the kinds of ideals they believe in. The very best but also the most satanic manifestations of man's mind are expressions not of his flesh but of this "idealism" of his spirit. Therefore a relativistic view which claims that to have some ideal or some religious feeling is valuable in itself is dangerous and erroneous. We must understand every ideal including those which appear in secular ideologies as expressions of the same human need and we must judge them with respect to their truth, to the extent to which they are conducive to the unfolding of man's powers and to the degree to which they are a real answer to man's need for equilibrium and harmony in his world. We repeat then that the understanding of human motivation must proceed from the understanding of the human situation.

2. Personality

Men are alike, for they share the human situation and its inherent existential dichotomies; they are unique in the specific way they solve their human problem. The infinite diversity of personalities is in itself characteristic of human existence.

By personality I understand the totality of inherited and acquired psychic qualities which are characteristic of one individual and which make the individual unique. The difference between inherited and acquired qualities is on the whole synonymous with the difference between temperament, gifts, and all constitutionally given psychic qualities on the one hand and character on the other. While differences in temperament have no ethical significance, differences in character constitute the real problem of ethics; they are expressive of the degree to which an individual has succeeded in the art of living. In order to avoid the confusion which prevails in the usage of the terms "temperament" and "character" we shall begin with a brief discussion of temperament.

A. TEMPERAMENT

Hippocrates distinguished four temperaments: choleric, sanguine, melancholic, and phlegmatic. The sanguine and choleric temperaments are modes of reaction which are characterized by easy excitability and quick alternation of interest, the interests being feeble in the former and intense in the latter. The phlegmatic and melancholic temperaments, on the contrary, are characterized by persistent but slow excitability of interest, the interest in the phlegmatic being feeble and in the melancholic intense.[2] In Hippocrates' view, these different modes of reaction were connected with different somatic sources. (It is interesting to note that in popular usage only the negative aspects of these temperaments are remembered:

[2] The four temperaments were symbolized by the four elements: choleric = fire = warm and dry, quick and strong; sanguine = air = warm and moist, quick and weak; phlegmatic = water = cold and moist, slow and weak; melancholic = earth = cold and dry, slow and strong.

choleric today means easily angered; melancholic, depressed; sanguine, overoptimistic; and phlegmatic, too slow.) These categories of temperament were used by most students of temperament until the time of Wundt. The most important modern concepts of types of temperament are those of Jung, Kretschmer, and Sheldon.[3]

Of the importance of further research in this field, particularly with regard to the correlation of temperament and somatic processes, there can be no doubt. But it will be necessary to distinguish clearly between character and temperament because the confusion of the two concepts has blocked progress in characterology as well as in the study of temperament.

Temperament refers to the *mode* of reaction and is constitutional and not changeable; character is essentially formed by a person's experiences, especially of those in early life, and changeable, to some extent, by insights and new kinds of experiences. If a person has a choleric temperament, for instance, his mode of reaction is "quick and strong." But what he is quick and strong *about* depends on his kind of relatedness, his character. If he is a productive, just, loving person he will react quickly and strongly when he loves, when he is enraged by injustice, and when he is impressed by a new idea. If he is a destructive or sadistic character he will be quick and strong in his destructiveness or in his cruelty.

The confusion between temperament and character has had serious consequences for ethical theory. Preferences with regard to differences in temperament are mere matters of subjective taste. But differences in character are ethically of the most fundamental importance. An example may help to clarify this point. Goering and Himmler

[3] Cf. also Charles William Morris' application of types of temperament to cultural entities in *Paths of Life* (New York: Harper & Brothers, 1942).

were men of different temperaments—the former
a cyclothyme, the latter a schizothyme. Hence,
from the standpoint of a subjective preference, an
individual who is attracted by the cyclothymic
temperament would have "liked" Goering better
than Himmler, and vice versa. However, from the
standpoint of character, both men had one quality
in common: they were ambitious sadists. Hence,
from an ethical standpoint they were equally evil.
Conversely, among productive characters, one
might subjectively prefer a choleric to a sanguine
temperament; but such judgments would not constitute judgments of the respective value of the
two people.[4]

In the application of C. G. Jung's concepts of
temperament, those of "introvert" and "extrovert," we often find the same confusion. Those
who prefer the extrovert tend to describe the

[4] An indication of the confusion between temperament
and character is the fact that Kretschmer, although
generally consistent in the usage of the concept of temperament, gave his book the title *Physique and Character*
instead of "Temperament and Physique." *Sheldon*, whose
book has the title of *Varieties of Temperament*, is nevertheless confused in the clinical application of his temperament concept. His "temperaments" contain pure traits of
temperament mixed with traits of character as they appear
in persons of a certain temperament. If the majority of
subjects had not reached full emotional maturity, certain
temperament types among them will show certain character
traits which have an affinity with this temperament. A
case in point is the trait of indiscriminate sociability
which Sheldon lists as one among the traits in the
viscerotonic temperament. But only the immature, nonproductive viscerotonic will have an indiscriminate sociability; the productive viscerotonic will have a discriminate
sociability. The trait listed by Sheldon is not a temperament trait but a character trait which appears frequently
associated with a certain temperament and physique provided that most subjects belong to the same level of maturity. Since Sheldon's method is one of relying entirely
on statistical correlation of "traits" with physique, with
no attempt at a theoretical analysis of the trait syndrome,
his mistake was hardly avoidable.

introvert as inhibited and neurotic; those who
prefer the introvert describe the extrovert as
superficial and lacking in perseverance and depth.
The fallacy is to compare a "good" person of one
temperament with a "bad" person of another
temperament, and to ascribe the difference in
value to the difference in temperament.

I think it is evident how this confusion between
temperament and character has affected ethics.
For, while it has led to condemnation of whole
races whose predominant temperaments differ
from our own, it has also supported relativism by
the assumption that differences in character are
as much differences in taste as those of temperament.

For purposes of discussing ethical theory, then,
we must turn to the concept of character, which
is both the subject matter of ethical judgment and
the object of man's ethical development. And here,
too, we must first clear the ground of traditional
confusions which, in this case, center around the
differences between the dynamic and the behavioristic concept of character.

B. CHARACTER

(1) The Dynamic Concept of Character

Character traits were and are considered by
behavioristically orientated psychologists to be
synonymous with behavior traits. From this standpoint character is defined as "the pattern of behavior characteristic for a given individual,"[5]
while other authors like William McDougall, R. G.
Gordon, and Kretschmer have emphasized the
conative and dynamic element of character traits.

Freud developed not only the first but also the

[5] Leland E. Hinsie and Jacob Shatzky, *Psychiatric
Dictionary*. (New York: Oxford University Press, 1940.)

most consistent and penetrating theory of character as a system of strivings which underlie, but are not identical with, behavior. In order to appreciate Freud's dynamic concept of character, a comparison between behavior traits and character traits will be helpful. Behavior traits are described in terms of actions which are observable by a third person. Thus, for instance, the behavior trait "being courageous" would be defined as behavior which is directed toward reaching a certain goal without being deterred by risks to one's comfort, freedom, or life. Or parsimony as a behavior trait would be defined as behavior which aims at saving money or other material things. However, if we inquire into the motivation and particularly into the unconscious motivation of such behavior traits we find that the behavior trait covers numerous and entirely different character traits. Courageous behavior may be motivated by ambition so that a person will risk his life in certain situations in order to satisfy his craving for being admired; it may be motivated by suicidal impulses which drive a person to seek danger because, consciously or unconsciously, he does not value his life and wants to destroy himself; it may be motivated by sheer lack of imagination so that a person acts courageously because he is not aware of the danger awaiting him; finally, it may be determined by genuine devotion to the idea or aim for which a person acts, a motivation which is conventionally assumed to be the basis of courage. Superficially the behavior in all these instances is the same in spite of the different motivations. I say "superficially" because if one can observe such behavior minutely one finds that the difference in motivation results also in subtle differences in behavior. An officer in battle, for instance, will behave quite differently in different situations if his courage is motivated by devotion to an idea rather than by ambition. In the first case he would not attack in certain situations if the risks are in no proportion to the tactical ends to be gained. If, on the other hand, he is driven by vanity, this passion may make him blind to the dangers threatening him and his soldiers. His behavior trait "courage" in the latter case is obviously a very ambiguous asset. Another illustration is parsimony. A person may be economical because his economic circumstances make it necessary; or he may be parsimonious because he has a stingy character, which makes saving an aim for its own sake regardless of the realistic necessity. Here, too, the motivation would make some difference with regard to behavior itself. In the first case, the person would be very well able to discern a situation where it is wise to save from one in which it is wiser to spend money. In the latter case he will save regardless of the objective need for it. Another factor which is determined by the difference in motivation refers to the prediction of behavior. In the case of a "courageous" soldier motivated by ambition we may predict that he will behave courageously only if his courage can be rewarded. In the case of the soldier who is courageous because of devotion to his cause we can predict that the question of whether or not his courage will find recognition will have little influence on his behavior.

Closely related to Freud's concept of unconscious motivation is his theory of the conative nature of character traits. He recognized something that the great novelists and dramatists had always known: that, as Balzac put it, the study of character deals with "the forces by which man is motivated"; that the way a person acts, feels, and thinks is to a large extent determined by the specificity of his character and is not merely the result of rational responses to realistic situations; that "man's fate is his character." Freud recognized the dynamic quality of character traits and that the character structure of a person represents a particular form in which energy is canalized in the process of living.

Freud tried to account for this dynamic nature of character traits by combining his characterology with his libido theory. In accordance with the type of materialistic thinking prevalent in the natural sciences of the late nineteenth century, which assumed the energy in natural and psychical phenomena to be a substantial, not a relational entity, Freud believed that the sexual drive was the source of energy of the character. By a number of complicated and brilliant assumptions he explained different character traits as "sublimations" of, or "reaction formations" against, the various forms of the sexual drive. He interpreted the *dynamic nature* of character traits as an expression of their *libidinous source*.

The progress of psychoanalytic theory led, in line with the progress of the natural and social sciences, to a new concept which was based, not on the idea of a primarily isolated individual, but on the *relationship* of man to others, to nature, and to himself. It was assumed that this very relationship governs and regulates the energy manifest in the passionate strivings of man. H. S. Sullivan, one of the pioneers of this new view, has accordingly defined psychoanalysis as a "study of interpersonal relations."

The theory presented in the following pages follows Freud's characterology in essential points: in the assumption that character traits underlie behavior and must be inferred from it; that they constitute forces which, though powerful, the person may be entirely unconscious of. It follows Freud also in the assumption that the fundamental entity in character is not the single character trait but the total character organization from which a number of single character traits follow. These character traits are to be understood as a syndrome which results from a particular organization or, as I shall call it, orientation of character. I shall deal only with a very limited number of character traits which follow immediately from the underlying orientation. A number of other character traits could be dealt with similarly, and it could be shown that they are also direct outcomes of basic orientations or mixtures of such primary traits of character with those of temperament. However, a great number of others conventionally listed as character traits would be found to be not character traits in our sense but pure temperament or mere behavior traits.

The main difference in the theory of character proposed here from that of Freud is that the fundamental basis of character is not seen in various types of libido organization but in specific kinds of a person's relatedness to the world. In the process of living, man relates himself to the world (1) by acquiring and assimilating things, and (2) by relating himself to people (and himself). The former I shall call the process of assimilation; the latter, that of socialization. Both forms of relatedness are "open" and not, as with the animal, instinctively determined. Man can acquire things by receiving or taking them from an outside source or by producing them through his own effort. But he must acquire and assimilate them in some fashion in order to satisfy his needs. Also, man cannot live alone and unrelated to others. He has to associate with others for defense, for work, for sexual satisfaction, for play, for the upbringing of the young, for the transmission of knowledge and material possessions. But beyond that, it is necessary for him to be related to others, one with them, part of a group. Complete isolation is unbearable and incompatible with sanity. Again man can relate himself to others in various ways: he can love or hate, he can compete or cooperate; he can build a social system based on equality or authority, liberty or oppression; but he must be related in some fashion and the particular form of relatedness is expressive of his character.

These orientations, by which the individual relates himself to the world, constitute the core of his character; character can be defined as the *(relatively permanent) form in which human energy is canalized in the process of assimilation and socialization.* This canalization of psychic energy has a very significant biological function. Since man's actions are not determined by innate instinctual patterns, life would be precarious, indeed, if he had to make a deliberate decision each time he acted, each time he took a step. On the contrary, many actions must be performed far more quickly than conscious deliberation allows. Furthermore, if all behavior followed from deliberate decision, many more inconsistencies in action would occur than are compatible with proper functioning. According to behavioristic thinking, man learns to react in a semiautomatic fashion by developing habits of action and thought which can be understood in terms of conditioned reflexes. While this view is correct to a certain extent, it ignores the fact that the most deeply rooted habits and opinions which are characteristic of a person and resistant to change grow from his character structure: they are expressive of the particular form in which energy has been canalized in the character structure. The character system can be considered the human substitute for the instinctive apparatus of the animal. Once energy is canalized in a certain way, action takes place "true to character." A particular character may be undesirable ethically, but at least it permits a person to act fairly consistently and to be relieved of the burden of having to make a new and deliberate decision every time. He can arrange his life in a way which is geared to his character and thus create a certain degree of compatibility between the inner and the outer situation. Moreover, character has also a selective function with regard to a person's ideas and values. Since to most people ideas seem to be independent of their emotions and wishes and the result of logical deduction, they feel that their attitude toward the world is confirmed by their ideas and judgments when actually these are as much a result of their character as their actions are. This confirmation in turn tends to stabilize their character structure since it makes the latter appear right and sensible.

Not only has character the function of permitting the individual to act consistently and "reasonably"; it is also the basis for his adjustment to society. The character of the child is molded by the character of its parents in response to whom it develops. The parents and their methods of child training in turn are determined by the social structure of their culture. The average family is the "psychic agency" of society, and by adjusting himself to his family the child acquires the character which later makes him adjusted to the tasks he has to perform in social life. He acquires that character which makes him want to do what he has to do and the core of which he shares with most members of the same social class or culture. The fact that most members of a social class or culture share significant elements of character and that one can speak of a "social character" representing the core of a character structure common to most people of a given culture shows the degree to which character is formed by social and cultural patterns. But from the social character we must differentiate the individual character in which one person differs from another within the same culture. These differences are partly due to the differences of the personalities of the parents and to the differences, psychic and material, of the specific social environment in which the child grows up. But they are also due to the constitutional differences of each individual, particularly those of temperament. Genetically, the formation of individual character is determined by the impact of its life experiences, the individual ones and those which follow from the culture, on temperament and physical constitution. Environment is never the same for two people, for the difference in constitution makes them experience the same environment in a more or less different way. Mere habits of action and thought which develop as the result of an individual's conforming with the cultural pattern and which are not rooted in the character of a person are easily changed under the influence of new social patterns. If, on the other hand, a person's behavior is rooted in his character, it is charged with energy and changeable only if a fundamental change in a person's character takes place.

In the following analysis *nonproductive orientations* are differentiated from the *productive orientation*.[6] It must be noted that these concepts are "ideal-types," not descriptions of the character of a given individual. Furthermore, while, for didactic purposes, they are treated here separately, the character of any given person is usually a blend of all or some of these orientations in which one, however, is dominant. Finally, I want to state here that in the description of the nonproductive orientations only their negative aspects are presented, while their positive aspects are discussed briefly in a later part of this chapter.[7]

---

[6] If the reader wishes to begin with a picture of all the types, he can turn to the diagram on p. 116.

[7] See pp. 117 ff. The following description of the nonproductive orientations, except that of the marketing, follows the clinical picture of the pregenital character given by Freud and others. The theoretical difference becomes apparent in the discussion of the hoarding character.

(2) Types of Character: The Nonproductive Orientations

(a) The Receptive Orientation

In the receptive orientation a person feels "the source of all good" to be outside, and he believes that the only way to get what he wants—be it something material, be it affection, love, knowledge, pleasure—is to receive it from that outside source. In this orientation the problem of love is almost exclusively that of "being loved" and not that of loving. Such people tend to be indiscriminate in the choice of their love objects, because being loved by anybody is such an overwhelming experience for them that they "fall for" anybody who gives them love or what looks like love. They are exceedingly sensitive to any withdrawal or rebuff they experience on the part of the loved person. Their orientation is the same in the sphere of thinking: if intelligent, they make the best listeners, since their orientation is one of receiving, not of producing, ideas; left to themselves, they feel paralyzed. It is characteristic of these people that their first thought is to find somebody else to give them needed information rather than to make even the smallest effort of their own. If religious, these persons have a concept of God in which they expect everything from God and nothing from their own activity. If not religious, their relationship to persons or institutions is very much the same; they are always in search of a "magic helper." They show a particular kind of loyalty, at the bottom of which is the gratitude for the hand that feeds them and the fear of ever losing it. Since they need many hands to feel secure, they have to be loyal to numerous people. It is difficult for them to say "no," and they are easily caught between conflicting loyalties and promises. Since they cannot say "no," they love to say "yes" to everything and everybody, and the resulting paralysis of their critical abilities makes them increasingly dependent on others.

They are dependent not only on authorities for knowledge and help but on people in general for any kind of support. They feel lost when alone because they feel that they cannot do anything without help. This helplessness is especially important with regard to those acts which by their very nature can only be done alone—making decisions and taking responsibility. In personal relationships, for instance, they ask advice from the very person with regard to whom they have to make a decision.

This receptive type has great fondness for food and drink. These persons tend to overcome anxiety and depression by eating or drinking. The mouth is an especially prominent feature, often the most expressive one; the lips tend to be open, as if in a state of continuous expectation of being fed. In their dreams, being fed is a frequent symbol of being loved; being starved, an expression of frustration or disappointment.

By and large, the outlook of people of this receptive orientation is optimistic and friendly; they have a certain confidence in life and its gifts, but they become anxious and distraught when their "source of supply" is threatened. They often have a genuine warmth and a wish to help others, but doing things for others also assumes the function of securing their favor.

(b) The Exploitative Orientation

The exploitative orientation, like the receptive, has as its basic premise the feeling that the source of all good is outside, that whatever one wants to get must be sought there, and that one cannot produce anything oneself. The difference between the two, however, is that the exploitative type does not expect to receive things from others as gifts, but to take them away from others by force or cunning. This orientation extends to all spheres of activity.

In the realm of love and affection these people tend to grab and steal. They feel attracted only to people whom they can take away from somebody else. Attractiveness to them is conditioned by a person's attachment to somebody else; they tend not to fall in love with an unattached person.

We find the same attitude with regard to thinking and intellectual pursuits. Such people will tend not to produce ideas but to steal them. This may be done directly in the form of plagiarism or more subtly by repeating in different phraseology the ideas voiced by others and insisting they are new and their own. It is a striking fact that frequently people with great intelligence proceed in this way, although if they relied on their own gifts they might well be able to have ideas of their own. The lack of original ideas or independent production in otherwise gifted people often has its explanation in this character orientation, rather than in any innate lack of originality. The same statement holds true with regard to their orientation to material things. Things which they can take away from others always seem better to them than anything they can produce themselves. They use and exploit anybody and anything from whom or from which they can squeeze something. Their motto is: "Stolen fruits are sweetest." Because they want to use and exploit people, they "love" those who, explicitly or implicitly, are promising objects of exploitation, and get "fed up" with persons whom they have squeezed out. An extreme example is the kleptomaniac who enjoys things only if he can steal them, although he has the money to buy them.

This orientation seems to be symbolized by the

biting mouth which is often a prominent feature in such people. It is not a play upon words to point out that they often make "biting" remarks about others. Their attitude is colored by a mixture of hostility and manipulation. Everyone is an object of exploitation and is judged according to his usefulness. Instead of the confidence and optimism which characterizes the receptive type, one finds here suspicion and cynicism, envy and jealousy. Since they are satisfied only with things they can take away from others, they tend to overrate what others have and underrate what is theirs.

(c) The Hoarding Orientation

While the receptive and exploitative types are similar inasmuch as both expect to get things from the outside world, the hoarding orientation is essentially different. This orientation makes people have little faith in anything new they might get from the outside world; their security is based upon hoarding and saving, while spending is felt to be a threat. They have surrounded themselves, as it were, by a protective wall, and their main aim is to bring as much as possible into this fortified position and to let as little as possible out of it. Their miserliness refers to money and material things as well as to feelings and thoughts. Love is essentially a possession; they do not give love but try to get it by possessing the "beloved." The hoarding person often shows a particular kind of faithfulness toward people and even toward memories. Their sentimentality makes the past appear as golden; they hold on to it and indulge in the memories of bygone feelings and experiences. They know everything but are sterile and incapable of productive thinking.

One can recognize these people too by facial expressions and gestures. Theirs is the tight-lipped mouth; their gestures are characteristic of their withdrawn attitude. While those of the receptive type are inviting and round, as it were, and the gestures of the exploitative type are aggressive and pointed, those of the hoarding type are angular, as if they wanted to emphasize the frontiers between themselves and the outside world. Another characteristic element in this attitude is pedantic orderliness. The hoarder will be orderly with things, thoughts, or feelings, but again, as with memory, his orderliness is sterile and rigid. He cannot endure things out of place and will automatically rearrange them. To him the outside world threatens to break into his fortified position; orderliness signifies mastering the world outside by putting it, and keeping it, in its proper place in order to avoid the danger of intrusion. His compulsive cleanliness is another expression of his need to undo contact with the outside world. Things beyond his own frontiers are felt to be dangerous and "unclean"; he annuls the menacing contact by compulsive washing, similar to a religious washing ritual prescribed after contact with unclean things or people. Things have to be put not only in their proper place but also into their proper time; obsessive punctuality is characteristic of the hoarding type; it is another form of mastering the outside world. If the outside world is experienced as a threat to one's fortified position, obstinacy is a logical reaction. A constant "no" is the almost automatic defense against intrusion; sitting tight, the answer to the danger of being pushed. These people tend to feel that they possess only a fixed quantity of strength, energy, or mental capacity, and that this stock is diminished or exhausted by use and can never be replenished. They cannot understand the self-replenishing function of all living substance and that activity and the use of one's powers increase strength while stagnation paralyzes; to them, death and destruction have more reality than life and growth. The act of creation is a miracle of which they hear but in which they do not believe. Their highest values are order and security; their motto: "There is nothing new under the sun." In their relationship to others intimacy is a threat; either remoteness or possession of a person means security. The hoarder tends to be suspicious and to have a particular sense of justice which in effect says: "Mine is mine and yours is yours."

(d) The Marketing Orientation

The marketing orientation developed as a dominant one only in the modern era. In order to understand its nature one must consider the economic function of the market in modern society as being not only analogous to this character orientation but as the basis and the main condition for its development in modern man.

Barter is one of the oldest economic mechanisms. The traditional local market, however, is essentially different from the market as it has developed in modern capitalism. Bartering on a local market offered an opportunity to meet for the purpose of exchanging commodities. Producers and customers became acquainted; they were relatively small groups; the demand was more or less known, so that the producer could produce for this specific demand.

The modern market[8] is no longer a meeting place but a mechanism characterized by abstract and impersonal demand. One produces for this market, not for a known circle of customers; its verdict is based on laws of supply and demand; and it determines whether the commodity can be sold and at what price. No matter what the *use*

[8] Cf., for the study of history and function of the modern market, K. Polanyi's *The Great Transformation* (New York: Rinehart & Company, 1944).

value of a pair of shoes may be, for instance, if the supply is greater than the demand, some shoes will be sentenced to economic death; they might as well not have been produced at all. The market day is the "day of judgment" as far as the *exchange value* of commodities is concerned.

The reader may object that this description of the market is oversimplified. The producer does try to judge the demand in advance, and under monopoly conditions even obtains a certain degree of control over it. Nevertheless, the regulatory function of the market has been, and still is, predominant enough to have a profound influence on the character formation of the urban middle class and, through the latter's social and cultural influence, on the whole population. The market concept of value, the emphasis on exchange value rather than on use value, has led to a similar concept of value with regard to people and particularly to oneself. The character orientation which is rooted in the experience of oneself as a commodity and of one's value as exchange value I call the marketing orientation.

In our time the marketing orientation has been growing rapidly, together with the development of a new market that is a phenomenon of the last decades—the "personality market." Clerks and salesmen, business executives and doctors, lawyers and artists all appear on this market. It is true that their legal status and economic positions are different: some are independent, charging for their services; others are employed, receiving salaries. But all are dependent for their material success on a personal acceptance by those who need their services or who employ them.

The principle of evaluation is the same on both the personality and the commodity market: on the one, personalities are offered for sale; on the other, commodities. Value in both cases is their exchange value, for which use value is a necessary but not a sufficient condition. It is true, our economic system could not function if people were not skilled in the particular work they have to perform and were gifted only with a pleasant personality. Even the best bedside manner and the most beautifully equipped office on Park Avenue would not make a New York doctor successful if he did not have a minimum of medical knowledge and skill. Even the most winning personality would not prevent a secretary from losing her job unless she could type reasonably fast. However, if we ask what the respective weight of skill and personality as a condition for success is, we find that only in exceptional cases is success predominantly the result of skill and of certain other human qualities like honesty, decency, and integrity. Although the proportion between skill and human qualities on the one hand and "personality" on the other hand as prerequisites for success varies, the "personality factor" always plays a decisive role. Success depends largely on how well a person sells himself on the market, how well he gets his personality across, how nice a "package" he is; whether he is "cheerful," "sound," "aggressive," "reliable," "ambitious"; furthermore what his family background is, what clubs he belongs to, and whether he knows the right people. The type of personality required depends to some degree on the special field in which a person works. A stockbroker, a salesman, a secretary, a railroad executive, a college professor, or a hotel manager must each offer different kinds of personality that, regardless of their differences, must fulfill one condition: to be in demand.

The fact that in order to have success it is not sufficient to have the skill and equipment for performing a given task but that one must be able to "put across" one's personality in competition with many others shapes the attitude toward oneself. If it were enough for the purpose of making a living to rely on what one knows and what one can do, one's self-esteem would be in proportion to one's capacities, that is, to one's use value; but since success depends largely on how one sells one's personality, one experiences oneself as a commodity or rather simultaneously as the seller *and* the commodity to be sold. A person is not concerned with his life and happiness, but with becoming salable. This feeling might be compared to that of a commodity, of handbags on a counter, for instance, could they feel and think. Each handbag would try to make itself as "attractive" as possible in order to attract customers and to look as expensive as possible in order to obtain a higher price than its rivals. The handbag sold for the highest price would feel elated, since that would mean it was the most "valuable" one; the one which was not sold would feel sad and convinced of its own worthlessness. This fate might befall a bag which, though excellent in appearance and usefulness, had the bad luck to be out of date because of a change in fashion.

Like the handbag, one has to be in fashion on the personality market, and in order to be in fashion one has to know what kind of personality is most in demand. This knowledge is transmitted in a general way throughout the whole process of education, from kindergarten to college, and implemented by the family. The knowledge acquired at this early stage is not sufficient, however; it emphasizes only certain general qualities like adaptability, ambition, and sensitivity to the changing expectations of other people. The more specific picture of the models for success one gets elsewhere. The pictorial magazines, newspapers, and newsreels show the pictures and life stories of the successful in many variations. Pictorial advertising has a similar function. The successful executive who is pictured in a tailor's advertisement is the image of how one should look and be, if one is to draw down the "big money" on the contemporary personality market.

The most important means of transmitting the desired personality pattern to the average man is the motion picture. The young girl tries to emulate the facial expression, coiffure, gestures of a high-priced star as the most promising way to success. The young man tries to look and be like the model he sees on the screen. While the average citizen has little contact with the life of the most successful people, his relationship with the motion-picture stars is different. It is true that he has no real contact with them either, but he can see them on the screen again and again, can write to them and receive their autographed pictures. In contrast to the time when the actor was socially despised but was nevertheless the transmitter of the works of great poets to his audience, our motion-picture stars have no great works or ideas to transmit, but their function is to serve as the link an average person has with the world of the "great." Even if he can not hope to become as successful as they are, he can try to emulate them; they are his saints and because of their success they embody the norms for living.

Since modern man experiences himself both as the seller and as the commodity to be sold on the market, his self-esteem depends on conditions beyond his control. If he is "successful," he is valuable; if he is not, he is worthless. The degree of insecurity which results from this orientation can hardly be overestimated. If one feels that one's own value is not constituted primarily by the human qualities one possesses, but by one's success on a competitive market with ever-changing conditions, one's self-esteem is bound to be shaky and in constant need of confirmation by others. Hence one is driven to strive relentlessly for success, and any setback is a severe threat to one's self-esteem; helplessness, insecurity, and inferiority feelings are the result. If the vicissitudes of the market are the judges of one's value, the sense of dignity and pride is destroyed.

But the problem is not only that of self-evaluation and self-esteem but of one's experience of oneself as an independent entity, of one's *identity with oneself.* As we shall see later, the mature and productive individual derives his feeling of identity from the experience of himself as the agent who is one with his powers; this feeling of self can be briefly expressed as meaning *"I am what I do."* In the marketing orientation man encounters his own powers as commodities alienated from him. He is not one with them but they are masked from him because what matters is not his self-realization in the process of using them but his success in the process of selling them. Both his powers and what they create become estranged, something different from himself, something for others to judge and to use; thus his feeling of identity becomes as shaky as his self-esteem; it is constituted by the sum total of roles one can play: *"I am as you desire me."*

Ibsen has expressed this state of selfhood in Peer Gynt: Peer Gynt tries to discover his self and he finds that he is like an onion—one layer after the other can be peeled off and there is no core to be found. Since man cannot live doubting his identity, he must, in the marketing orientation, find the conviction of identity not in reference to himself and his powers but in the opinion of others about him. His prestige, status, success, the fact that he is known to others as being a certain person are a substitute for the genuine feeling of identity. This situation makes him utterly dependent on the way others look at him and forces him to keep up the role in which he once had become successful. If I and my powers are separated from each other, then, indeed, is my self constituted by the price I fetch.

The way one experiences others is not different from the way one experiences oneself.[9] Others are experienced as commodities like oneself; they too do not present *themselves* but their salable part. The difference between people is reduced to a merely quantitative difference of being *more or less* successful, attractive, hence valuable. This process is not different from what happens to commodities on the market. A painting and a pair of shoes can both be expressed in, and reduced to, their exchange value, their price; so many pairs of shoes are "equal" to one painting. In the same way the difference between people is reduced to a common element, their price on the market. Their individuality, that which is peculiar and unique in them, is valueless and, in fact, a ballast. The meaning which the word *peculiar* has assumed is quite expressive of this attitude. Instead of denoting the greatest achievement of man— that of having developed his individuality— it has become almost synonymous with *queer*. The word *equality* has also changed its meaning. The idea that all men are created equal implied that all men have the same fundamental right to be considered as ends in themselves and not as means. Today, equality has become equivalent to *interchangeability*, and is the very negation of individuality. Equality, instead of being the condition for the development of each man's peculiarity, means the extinction of individuality, the "selflessness" characteristic of the marketing orientation. Equality was conjunctive with difference, but it has become synonymous with "indifference" and, indeed, indifference is what characterizes modern man's relationship to himself and to others.

These conditions necessarily color all human

[9] The fact that relationship to oneself and to others is conjunctive will be explained in Chapter IV.

relationships. When the individual self is neglected, the relationships between people must of
necessity become superficial, because not they
themselves but interchangeable commodities are
related. People are not able and cannot afford to
be concerned with that which is unique and "peculiar" in each other. However, the market creates
a kind of comradeship of its own. Everybody is involved in the same battle of competition, shares the
same striving for success; all meet under the same
conditions of the market (or at least believe they
do). Everyone knows how the others feel because
each is in the same boat: alone, afraid to fail,
eager to please; no quarter is given or expected
in this battle.

The superficial character of human relationships leads many to hope that they can find depth
and intensity of feeling in individual love. But love
for one person and love for one's neighbor are
indivisible; in any given culture, love relationships
are only a more intense expression of the relatedness to man prevalent in that culture. Hence it is
an illusion to expect that the loneliness of man
rooted in the marketing orientation can be cured
by individual love.

Thinking as well as feeling is determined by the
marketing orientation. Thinking assumes the
function of grasping things quickly so as to be able
to manipulate them successfully. Furthered by
widespread and efficient education, this leads to a
high degree of intelligence, but not of reason.[10]
For manipulative purposes, all that is necessary
to know is the surface features of things, the
superficial. The truth, to be uncovered by penetrating to the essence of phenomena, becomes an
obsolete concept—truth not only in the pre-
scientific sense of "absolute" truth, dogmatically

[10] The difference between intelligence and reason will be
discussed later on, pp. 102 ff.

maintained without reference to empirical data, but also in the sense of truth attained by man's reason applied to his observations and open to revisions. Most intelligence tests are attuned to this kind of thinking; they measure not so much the capacity for reason and understanding as the capacity for quick mental adaptation to a given situation; "mental adjustment tests" would be the adequate name for them.[11] For this kind of thinking the application of the categories of comparison and of quantitative measurement—rather than a thorough analysis of a given phenomenon and its quality—is essential. All problems are equally "interesting" and there is little sense of the respective differences in their importance. Knowledge itself becomes a commodity. Here, too, man is alienated from his own power; thinking and knowing are experienced as a tool to produce results. Knowledge of man himself, psychology, which in the great tradition of Western thought was held to be the condition for virtue, for right living, for happiness, has degenerated into an instrument to be used for better manipulation of others and oneself, in market research, in political propaganda, in advertising, and so on.

Evidently this type of thinking has a profound effect on our educational system. From grade school to graduate school, the aim of learning is to gather as much information as possible that is mainly useful for the purposes of the market. Students are supposed to learn so many things that they have hardly time and energy left to *think*. Not the interest in the subjects taught or in knowledge and insight as such, but the enhanced exchange value knowledge gives is the main incentive for wanting more and better edu-

[11] Cf. Ernest Schachtel, "Zum Begriff und zur Diagnosis der Persoenlichkeit in 'Personality Tests' [On the Concept and Diagnosis of Personality Tests]," *Zeitschrift, fuer Sozialforschung* (Jahrgang 6, 1937), pp. 597–624.

cation. We find today a tremendous enthusiasm for knowledge and education, but at the same time a skeptical or contemptuous attitude toward the allegedly impractical and useless thinking which is concerned "only" with the truth and which has no exchange value on the market.

Although I have presented the marketing orientation as one of the nonproductive orientations, it is in many ways so different that it belongs in a category of its own. The receptive, exploitative, and hoarding orientations have one thing in common: each is one form of human relatedness which, if dominant in a person, is specific of him and characterizes him. (Later on it will be shown that these four orientations do not necessarily have the negative qualities which have been described so far.[12]) The marketing orientation, however, does not develop something which is potentially in the person (unless we make the absurd assertion that "nothing" is also part of the human equipment); its very nature is that no specific and permanent kind of relatedness is developed, but that the very changeability of attitudes is the only permanent quality of such orientation. In this orientation, those qualities are developed which can best be sold. Not one particular attitude is predominant, but the emptiness which can be filled most quickly with the desired quality. This quality, however, ceases to be one in the proper sense of the word; it is only a role, the pretense of a quality, to be readily exchanged if another one is more desirable. Thus, for instance, respectability is sometimes desirable. The salesmen in certain branches of business ought to impress the public with those qualities of reliability, soberness, and respectability which were genuine in many a businessman of the nineteenth century. Now one looks for a man who instills confidence because he

[12] Pp. 117 ff.

looks as if he had these qualities; what this man sells on the personality market is his ability to look the part; what kind of person is behind that role does not matter and is nobody's concern. He himself is not interested in his honesty, but in what it gets for him on the market. The premise of the marketing orientation is emptiness, the lack of any specific quality which could not be subject to change, since any persistent trait of character might conflict some day with the requirements of the market. Some roles would not fit in with the peculiarities of the person; therefore we must do away with them—not with the roles but with the peculiarities. The marketing personality must be free, free of all individuality.

The character orientations which have been described so far are by no means as separate from one another as it may appear from this sketch. The receptive orientation, for instance, may be dominant in a person but it is usually blended with any or all of the other orientations. While I shall discuss the various blendings later on in this chapter, I want to stress at this point that all orientations are part of the human equipment, and the dominance of any specific orientation depends to a large extent on the peculiarity of the culture in which the individual lives. Although a more detailed analysis of the relationship between the various orientations and social patterns must be reserved for a study which deals primarily with problems of social psychology, I should like to suggest here a tentative hypothesis as to the social conditions making for the dominance of any of the four nonproductive types. It should be noted that the significance of the study of the correlation between character orientation and social structure lies not only in the fact that it helps us understand some of the most significant causes for the formation of character, but also in the fact that specific orientations—inasmuch as they are common to most members of a culture or social class—represent powerful emotional forces the operation of which we must know in order to understand the functioning of society. In view of the current emphasis on the impact of culture on personality, I should like to state that the relationship between society and the individual is not to be understood simply in the sense that cultural patterns and social institutions "influence" the individual. The interaction goes much deeper; the whole personality of the average individual is molded by the way people relate to each other, and it is determined by the socioeconomic and political structure of society to such an extent that, in principle, one can infer from the analysis of one individual the totality of the social structure in which he lives.

The receptive orientation is often to be found in societies in which the right of one group to exploit another is firmly established. Since the exploited group has no power to change, or any idea of changing, its situation, it will tend to look up to its masters as to its providers, as to those from whom one receives everything life can give. No matter how little the slave receives, he feels that by his own effort he could have acquired even less, since the structure of his society impresses him with the fact that he is unable to organize it and to rely on his own activity and reason. As far as contemporary American culture is concerned, it seems at first glance that the receptive attitude is entirely absent. Our whole culture, its ideas, and its practice discourage the receptive orientation and emphasize that each one has to look out, and be responsible, for himself and that he has to use his own initiative if he wants to "get anywhere." However, while the receptive orientation is discouraged, it is by no means absent. The need to conform and to please, which has been discussed in the foregoing pages, leads to the feeling of helplessness, which is the root of subtle receptiveness in modern man. It appears particularly in the attitude toward the "expert" and public opinion. People expect that in every field there is an expert who can tell them how things are and how they ought to be done, and that all they ought to do is listen to him and swallow his ideas. There are experts for science, experts for happiness, and writers become experts in the art of living by the very fact that they are authors of best sellers. This subtle but rather general receptiveness assumes somewhat grotesque forms in modern "folklore," fostered particularly by advertising. While everyone knows that realistically the "get-rich-quick" schemes do not work, there is a widespread daydream of the effortless life. It is partly expressed in connection with the use of gadgets; the car which needs no shifting, the fountain pen which saves the trouble of removing the cap are only random examples of this fantasy. It is particularly prevalent in those schemes which deal with happiness. A very characteristic quotation is the following: "This book," the author says, "tells you how to be twice the man or woman you ever were before—happy, well, brimming with energy, confident, capable and free of care. You are required to follow no laborious mental or physical program; it is much simpler than that. . . . As laid down here the route to that promised profit may appear strange, for few of us can imagine *getting without striving.* . . . Yet that is so, as you will see."[13]

The exploitative character, with its motto "I take what I need," goes back to piratical and feudal ancestors and goes forward from there to the robber barons of the nineteenth century who exploited the natural resources of the continent.

[13] Hal·Falvey, *Ten Seconds That Will Change Your Life* (Chicago: Wilcox & Follett, 1946).

The "pariah" and "adventure" capitalists, to use Max Weber's terms, roaming the earth for profit, are men of this stamp, men whose aim was to buy cheap and sell dear and who ruthlessly pursued power and wealth. The free market as it operated in the eighteenth and nineteenth centuries under competitive conditions nurtured this type. Our own age has seen a revival of naked exploitativeness in the authoritarian systems which attempted to exploit the natural and human resources, not so much of their own country but of any other country they were powerful enough to invade. They proclaimed the right of might and rationalized it by pointing to the law of nature which makes the stronger survive; love and decency were signs of weakness; thinking was the occupation of cowards and degenerates.

The hoarding orientation existed side by side with the exploitative orientation in the eighteenth and nineteenth centuries. The hoarding type was conservative, less interested in ruthless acquisition than in methodical economic pursuits, based on sound principles and on the preservation of what had been acquired. To him property was a symbol of his self and its protection a supreme value. This orientation gave him a great deal of security; his possession of property and family, protected as they were by the relatively stable conditions of the nineteenth century, constituted a safe and manageable world. Puritan ethics, with the emphasis on work and success as evidence of goodness, supported the feeling of security and tended to give life meaning and a religious sense of fulfillment. This combination of a stable world, stable possessions, and a stable ethic gave the members of the middle class a feeling of belonging, self-confidence, and pride.

The marketing orientation does not come out of the eighteenth or nineteenth centuries; it is definitely a modern product. It is only recently that the package, the label, the brand name have become important, in people as well as in commodities. The gospel of working loses weight and the gospel of selling becomes paramount. In feudal times, social mobility was exceedingly limited and one could not use one's personality to get ahead. In the days of the competitive market, social mobility was relatively great, especially in the United States; if one "delivered the goods" one could get ahead. Today, the opportunities for the lone individual who can make a fortune all by himself are, in comparison with the previous period, greatly diminished. He who wants to get ahead has to fit into large organizations, and his ability to play the expected role is one of his main assets.

The depersonalization, the emptiness, the meaninglessness of life, the automatization of the individual result in a growing dissatisfaction and in a need to search for a more adequate way of living and for norms which could guide man to this end. The productive orientation which I am going to discuss now points to the type of character in whom growth and the development of all his potentialities is the aim to which all other activities are subordinated.

(3) The Productive Orientation

(a) General Characteristics

From the time of classic and medieval literature up to the end of the nineteenth century a great deal of effort was expended in describing the vision of what the good man and the good society ought to be. Such ideas were expressed partly in the form of philosophical or theological treatises, partly in the form of utopias. The twentieth century is conspicuous for the absence of such visions. The emphasis is on critical analysis of man and society, in which positive visions of what man ought to be are only implied. While there is no doubt that this criticism is of utmost significance and a condition for any improvement of society, the absence of visions projecting a "better" man and a "better" society has had the effect of paralyzing man's faith in himself and his future (and is at the same time the result of such a paralysis).

Contemporary psychology and particularly psychoanalysis are no exception in this respect. Freud and his followers have given a splendid analysis of the neurotic character. Their clinical description of the nonproductive character (in Freud's terms, the pregenital character) is exhaustive and accurate—quite regardless of the fact that the theoretical concepts they used are in need of revision. But the character of the normal, mature, healthy personality has found scarcely any consideration. This character, called the genital character by Freud, has remained a rather vague and abstract concept. It is defined by him as the character structure of a person in whom the oral and anal libido has lost its dominant position and functions under the supremacy of genital sexuality, the aim of which is sexual union with a member of the opposite sex. The description of the genital character does not go far beyond the statement that it is the character structure of an individual who is capable of functioning well sexually and socially.

In discussing the *productive character* I venture beyond critical analysis and inquire into the nature of the fully developed character that is the aim of human development and simultaneously the ideal of humanistic ethics. It may serve as a preliminary approach to the concept of productive orientation to state its connection with Freud's genital character. Indeed, if we do not use Freud's term literally in the context of his libido theory but *symbolically* it denotes quite accurately the meaning of productiveness. For the stage of sexual maturity is that in which man has the capacity of natural production; by the union of the sperm and the egg new life is produced. While this type of production is common to man and to animals, the capacity for material production is specific for man. Man is not only a rational and social animal. He can also be defined as a producing animal, capable of transforming the materials which he finds at hand, using his reason and imagination. Not only *can* he produce, he *must* produce in order to live. Material production, however, is but the most frequent symbol for productiveness as an aspect of character. The "productive orientation" [14] of personality refers to a fundamental attitude, a *mode of relatedness* in all realms of human experience. It covers mental, emotional, and sensory responses to others, to oneself, and to things. Productiveness is man's ability to use his powers and to realize the potentialities inherent in him. If we say *he* must use *his* powers we imply that he must be free and not dependent on someone who controls his powers. We imply, furthermore, that he is guided by reason, since he can make use of his powers only if he knows what they are, how to use them, and what to use them for. Productiveness means that he experiences himself as the embodiment of his powers and as the "actor"; that he feels himself one with his powers and at the same time that they are not masked and alienated from him.

In order to avoid the misunderstandings to which the term "productiveness" lends itself, it seems appropriate to discuss briefly what is not meant by productiveness.

Generally the word "productiveness" is associ-

---

[14] Productiveness as used in this book is meant as an expansion of the concept of spontaneity described in *Escape from Freedom.*

ated with creativeness, particularly artistic creativeness. The real artist, indeed, is the most
convincing representative of productiveness. But
not all artists are productive; a conventional
painting, e.g., may exhibit nothing more than the
technical skill to reproduce the likeness of a person in photographic fashion on a canvas. But a
person can experience, see, feel, and think productively without having the gift to create something visible or communicable. *Productiveness is
an attitude which every human being is capable of,
unless he is mentally and emotionally crippled.*

The term "productive" is also apt to be confused
with "active," and "productiveness" with "activity." While the two terms can be synonymous
(for instance, in Aristotle's concept of activity),
activity in modern usage frequently indicates the
very opposite of productiveness. Activity is usually defined as behavior which brings about a
change in an existing situation by an expenditure
of energy. In contrast, a person is described as
passive if he is unable to change or overtly influence an existing situation and is influenced or
moved by forces outside himself. This current concept of activity takes into account only the actual
expenditure of energy and the change brought
about by it. It does not distinguish between the
underlying psychic conditions governing the
activities.

An example, though an extreme one, of nonproductive activity is the activity of a person under
hypnosis. The person in a deep hypnotic trance
may have his eyes open, may walk, talk, and do
things; he "acts." The general definition of activity would apply to him, since energy is spent and
some change brought about. But if we consider
the particular character and quality of this activity, we find that it is not really the hypnotized
person who is the actor, but the hypnotist who, by
means of his suggestions, acts through him. While

the hypnotic trance is an artificial state, it is an extreme but characteristic example of a situation in which a person can be active and yet not be the true actor, his activity resulting from compelling forces over which he has no control.

A common type of nonproductive activity is the reaction to anxiety, whether acute or chronic, conscious or unconscious, which is frequently at the root of the frantic preoccupations of men today. Different from anxiety-motivated activity, though often blended with it, is the type of activity based on submission to or dependence on an authority. The authority may be feared, admired, or "loved" —usually all three are mixed—but the cause of the activity is the command of the authority, both in a formal way and with regard to its contents. The person is active because the authority wants him to be, and he does what the authority wants him to do. This kind of activity is found in the authoritarian character. To him activity means to act in the name of something higher than his own self. He can act in the name of God, the past, or duty, but not in the name of himself. The authoritarian character receives the impulse to act from a superior power which is neither assailable nor changeable, and is consequently unable to heed spontaneous impulses from within himself.[15]

Resembling submissive activity is automaton activity. Here we do not find dependence on overt authority, but rather on anonymous authority as it is represented by public opinion, culture patterns, common sense, or "science." The person feels or does what he is supposed to feel or do; his activity lacks spontaneity in the sense that it does

[15] But the authoritarian character does not only tend to submit but also wishes to dominate others. In fact, both the sadistic and the masochistic sides are always present, and they differ only in degree of their strength and their repression respectively. (See the discussion of the authoritarian character in *Escape from Freedom*, pp. 141 ff.)

not originate from his own mental or emotional experience but from an outside source.

Among the most powerful sources of activity are irrational passions. The person who is driven by stinginess, masochism, envy, jealousy, and all other forms of greed is compelled to act; yet his actions are neither free nor rational but in opposition to reason and to his interests as a human being. A person so obsessed repeats himself, becoming more and more inflexible, more and more stereotyped. He is active, but he is not productive.

Although the source of these activities is irrational and the acting persons are neither free nor rational, there can be important practical results, often leading to material success. In the concept of productiveness we are not concerned with activity *necessarily* leading to practical results but with an attitude, with a mode of reaction and orientation toward the world and oneself in the process of living. We are concerned with *man's character, not with his success.*[16]

Productiveness is man's realization of the potentialities characteristic of him, the use of his *powers*. But what is "power"? It is rather ironical that this word denotes two contradictory concepts: *power of* = capacity and *power over* = domination. This contradiction, however, is of a particular kind. Power = domination results from the paralysis of power = capacity. *"Power over" is the perversion of "power to."* The ability of man to make productive use of his powers is his po-

---

[16] An interesting although incomplete attempt to analyze productive thinking is Max Wertheimer's posthumously published work, *Productive Thinking* (New York: Harper & Brothers, 1945). Some of the aspects of productiveness are dealt with by Munsterberg, Natorp, Bergson, and James; in Brentano's and Husserl's analysis of the psychic "act"; in Dilthey's analysis of artistic production and in O. Schwarz, *Medizinische Anthropologie* (Leipzig: Hirzel, 1929), pp. iii ff. In all these works, however, the problem is not treated in relation to character.

tency; the inability is his impotence. With his power of reason he can penetrate the surface of phenomena and understand their essence. With his power of love he can break through the wall which separates one person from another. With his power of imagination he can visualize things not yet existing; he can plan and thus begin to create. Where potency is lacking, man's relatedness to the world is perverted into a desire to dominate, to exert power over others as though they were things. Domination is coupled with death, potency with life. Domination springs from impotence and in turn reinforces it, for if an individual can force somebody else to serve him, his own need to be productive is increasingly paralyzed.

How is man related to the world when he uses his powers productively?

The world outside oneself can be experienced in two ways: *reproductively* by perceiving actuality in the same fashion as a film makes a literal record of things photographed (although even mere reproductive perception requires the active participation of the mind) ; and *generatively* by conceiving it, by enlivening and re-creating this new material through the spontaneous activity of one's own mental and emotional powers. While to a certain extent everyone does react in both ways, the respective weight of each kind of experience differs widely. Sometimes either one of the two is atrophied, and the study of these extreme cases in which the reproductive or the generative mode is almost absent offers the best approach to the understanding of each of these phenomena.

The relative atrophy of the generative capacity is very frequent in our culture. A person may be able to recognize things as they are (or as his culture maintains them to be), but he is unable to enliven his perception from within. Such a person is the perfect "realist," who sees all there is to be seen of the surface features of phenomena but who is quite incapable of penetrating below the surface to the essential, and of visualizing what is not yet apparent. He sees the details but not the whole, the trees but not the forest. Reality to him is only the sum total of what has already materialized. This person is not lacking in imagination, but his is a calculating imagination, combining factors all of which are known and in existence, and inferring their future operation.

On the other hand, the person who has lost the capacity to perceive actuality is insane. The psychotic person builds up an inner world of reality in which he seems to have full confidence; he lives in his own world, and the common factors of reality as perceived by all men are unreal to him. When a person sees objects which do not exist in reality but are entirely the product of his imagination, he has hallucinations; he interprets events in terms of his own feelings, without reference to, or at least without proper acknowledgment of, what goes on in reality. A paranoid person may believe that he is being persecuted, and a chance remark may indicate a plan to humiliate and ruin him. He is convinced that the lack of any more obvious and explicit manifestation of such intention does not prove anything; that, although the remark may appear harmless on the surface, its real meaning becomes clear if one looks "deeper." For the psychotic person actual reality is wiped out and an inner reality has taken its place.

The "realist" sees only the surface features of things; he sees the manifest world, he can reproduce it photographically in his mind, and he can act by manipulating things and people as they appear in this picture. The insane person is incapable of seeing reality as it is; he perceives reality only as a symbol and a reflection of his inner world. Both are sick. The sickness of the psychotic who has lost contact with reality is such that he cannot function socially. The sickness of the "realist" impoverishes him as a human being. While he is not incapacitated in his social functioning, his view of reality is so distorted because of its lack of depth and perspective that he is apt to err when more than manipulation of immediately given data and short-range aims are involved. *"Realism" seems to be the very opposite of insanity and yet it is only its complement.*

The true opposite of both "realism" and insanity is productiveness. The normal human being is capable of relating himself to the world simultaneously by perceiving it as it is and by conceiving it enlivened and enriched by his own powers. If one of the two capacities is atrophied, man is sick; but the normal person has both capacities even though their respective weights differ. The presence of both reproductive and generative capacities is a precondition for productiveness; they are opposite poles whose interaction is the dynamic source of productiveness. With the last statement I want to emphasize that productiveness is not the sum or combination of both capacities but that it is something new which springs from this interaction.

We have described productiveness as a particular mode of relatedness to the world. The question arises whether there is anything which the productive person *produces* and if so, what? While it is true that man's productiveness can create material things, works of art, and systems of thought, *by far the most important object of productiveness is man himself.*

Birth is only one particular step in a continuum which begins with conception and ends with death. All that is between these two poles is a process of giving birth to one's potentialities, of bringing to life all that is potentially given in the two cells. But while physical growth proceeds by itself, if only the proper conditions are given, the process of birth on the mental plane, in contrast, does not occur automatically. It requires productive activity to give life to the emotional and intellectual potentialities of man, to give birth to his self. It is part of the tragedy of the human situation that the development of the self is never completed; even under the best conditions only part of man's potentialities is realized. Man always dies before he is fully born.

Although I do not intend to present a history of the concept of productiveness, I want to give some outstanding illustrations which may help to clarify the concept further. Productiveness is one of the key concepts in *Aristotle's* system of ethics. One can determine virtue, he says, by ascertaining the function of man. Just as in the case of a flute player, a sculptor, or any artist, the good is thought to reside in the specific function which distinguishes these men from others and makes them what they are, the good of man also resides in the specific function which distinguishes him from other species and makes him what he is. Such a function is an "*activity* of the soul which follows or implies a rational principle." [17] "But it makes perhaps no small difference," he says, "whether we place the chief good in possession or in use, in state of mind or activity. For the state of mind may exist without producing any good result, as in a man who is asleep or in some other way quite inactive, but the activity can not; for one who has the activity will of necessity be acting, and acting well." [18] The good man for Aristotle is the man who by his activity, under the guidance of his reason, brings to life the potentialities specific of man.

"By virtue and power," *Spinoza* says, "I understand the same thing." [19] Freedom and blessedness

[17] *Nicomachean Ethics*, 1098ᵃ, 8.
[18] *Ibid.*, 1098ᵇ, 32.
[19] Spinoza, *Ethics*, IV, Def. 8.

consist in man's understanding of himself and in
his effort to become that which he potentially is, to
approach "nearer and nearer to the model of human nature." [20] Virtue to Spinoza is identical with
the use of man's powers and vice is his failure to
use his power; the essence of evil for Spinoza is
impotence.[21]

In a poetic form the concept of productive activity has been expressed beautifully by Goethe
and by Ibsen. *Faust* is a symbol of man's eternal
search for the meaning of life. Neither science,
pleasure, nor might, not even beauty, answer
Faust's question. Goethe proposes that the only
answer to man's quest is productive activity,
which is identical with the good.

In the "Prologue in Heaven" the Lord says it is
not error which thwarts man but non-activity:

> "Man's active nature, flagging, seeks too soon to
>   level;
> Unqualified repose he learns to crave;
> Whence, willingly, the comrade him I gave,
> Who works, excites, and must create, as Devil.
> But ye, God's sons in love and duty,
> Enjoy the rich, the ever-living Beauty!
> *Creative Power*, that works eternal schemes,
> Clasp you in bonds of love, relaxing never,
> And what in wavering apparition gleams
> Fix in its place with thoughts that stand for-
>   ever!"[22]

At the end of the second part, Faust has won his
bet with Mephistopheles. He has erred and sinned,
but he has not committed the crucial sin—that of
unproductiveness. The last words of Faust express
this idea very clearly, symbolized by the act of
claiming tillable land from the sea:

[20] *Ibid.*, IV, Preface.
[21] *Ibid.*, IV, Def. 20.
[22] Bayard Taylor, tr. (Boston: Houghton Mifflin Co.)

"To many millions let me furnish soil,
  Though not secure, *yet free to active toil;*
  Green, fertile fields, where man and herds go
    forth,
  At once, with comfort, on the newest Earth,
  And swiftly settled on the hill's firm base,
  Created by the bold, industrious race.
  A land like Paradise here, round about:
  Up to the brink the tide may roar without,
  And though it gnaw, to burst with force the
    limit,
  By common impulse all unite to hem it.
  Yes! To this thought I hold with firm persis-
    tence;
  The last result of wisdom stamps it true:
  He only earns his freedom and existence,
  Who daily conquers them anew.
  Thus here, by dangers girt, shall glide away
  Of childhood, manhood, age, the vigorous day:
  And such a throng I fain would see,—
  Stand on free soil among a people free!
  Then dared I hail the Moment fleeing:
  'Ah, still delay—thou art so fair!'
  The traces cannot, of mine earthly being,
  In aeons perish,—they are there!—
  In proud fore-feeling of such lofty bliss,
  I now enjoy the highest Moment,—this!"[23]

While Goethe's Faust expresses the faith in
man which was characteristic of the progressive
thinkers of the eighteenth and nineteenth centuries, Ibsen's *Peer Gynt*—written in the second
half of the nineteenth century—is a critical
analysis of modern man and his unproductiveness.
The subtitle of the play might very well be
"Modern Man in Search of His Self." Peer Gynt
believes he is acting in behalf of his self when he
uses all his energy to make money and to become

---

[23] *Loc. cit.*, Part II, Act V.

successful. He lives according to the principle: "Be enough to thyself," represented by the Trolls, and not according to the human principle: "Be true to thyself." He discovers at the end of his life that his exploitativeness and egotism have prevented him from becoming himself, that the realization of the self is only possible if one is productive, if one can give birth to one's own potentialities. Peer Gynt's unrealized potentialities come to accuse him of his "sin" and point to the real cause of his human failure—his lack of productiveness.

> *The Threadballs* (on the ground)
> We are thoughts;
> You should have thought us;
> Little feet, to life
> You should have brought us!
> We should have risen
> With glorious sound;
> But here like threadballs
> We are earth-bound.
>
> *Withered Leaves*
> We are a watchword;
> You should have used us!
> Life, by your sloth,
> Has been refused us.
> By worms we're eaten
> All up and down;
> No fruit will have us
> For spreading crown.
>
> *A Sighing in the Air*
> We are songs;
> You should have sung us!
> In the depths of your heart
> Despair has wrung us!
> We lay and waited;
> You called us not.

> May your throat and voice
> With poison rot!

Dewdrops
> We are tears
> Which were never shed.
> The cutting ice
> Which all hearts dread
> We could have melted;
> But now its dart
> Is frozen into
> A stubborn heart.
> The wound is closed;
> Our power is lost.

Broken Straws
> We are deeds
> You have left undone;
> Strangled by doubt,
> Spoiled ere begun.
> At the Judgment Day
> We shall be there
> To tell our tale;
> How will you fare?[24]

Thus far we have devoted ourselves to an inquiry into the general characteristics of the
productive orientation. We must attempt now to
examine productiveness as it appears in specific
activities, since only by studying the concrete and
specific can one fully understand the general.

(b) Productive Love and Thinking

Human existence is characterized by the fact
that man is alone and separated from the world;
not being able to stand the separation, he is im-

[24] *Eleven Plays of Henrik Ibsen* (New York: The
Modern Library, Random House, Inc.), Act V, Scene VI.

pelled to seek for relatedness and oneness. There
are many ways in which he can realize this need,
but only one in which he, as a unique entity,
remains intact; only one in which his own powers
unfold in the very process of being related. It is
the paradox of human existence that man must
simultaneously seek for closeness and for independence; for oneness with others and at the same
time for the preservation of his uniqueness and
particularity.[25] As we have shown, the answer to
this paradox—and to the moral problem of man—
is *productiveness*.

One can be productively related to the world
by acting and by comprehending. Man *produces
things*, and in the process of creation he exercises
his powers over matter. Man *comprehends the
world*, mentally and emotionally, through love and
through reason. His power of reason enables him
to penetrate through the surface and to grasp
the essence of his object by getting into active
relation with it. His power of love enables him to
break through the wall which separates him from
another person and to comprehend him. Although
love and reason are only two different forms of
comprehending the world and although neither
is possible without the other, they are expressions
of different powers, that of emotion and that of
thinking, and hence must be discussed separately.

The concept of productive love is very different
indeed from what is frequently called love. There
is hardly any word which is more ambiguous and
confusing than the word "love." It is used to denote
almost every feeling short of hate and disgust. It
comprises everything from the love for ice cream

---

[25] This concept of relatedness as the synthesis of closeness and uniqueness is in many ways similar to the concept of "detached—attachment" in Charles Morris' *Paths
of Life* (New York: Harper & Brothers, 1942), one difference being that Morris' frame of reference is that of
temperament while mine is that of character.

to the love for a symphony, from mild sympathy
to the most intense feeling of closeness. People feel
they love if they have "fallen for" somebody. They
call their dependence love, and their possessiveness
too. They believe, in fact, that nothing is easier
than to love, that the difficulty lies only in finding
the right object, and that their failure to find
happiness in love is due to their bad luck in not
finding the right partner. But contrary to all this
confused and wishful thinking, love is a very
specific feeling; and while every human being has
a capacity for love, its realization is one of the
most difficult achievements. Genuine love is rooted
in productiveness and may properly be called,
therefore, "productive love." Its essence is the
same whether it is the mother's love for the child,
our love for man, or the erotic love between two
individuals. (That it is also the same with regard
to love for others and love for ourselves we shall
discuss later.)[26] Although the objects of love differ
and consequently the intensity and quality of love
itself differ, certain basic elements may be said
to be characteristic of all forms of productive
love. These are *care, responsibility, respect,* and
knowledge.

Care and responsibility denote that love is an
activity and not a passion by which one is overcome, nor an affect which one is "affected by."
The element of care and responsibility in productive love has been admirably described in the book
of Jonah. God has told Jonah to go to Nineveh
to warn its inhabitants that they will be punished
unless they mend their evil ways. Jonah runs away
from his mission because he is afraid that the
people in Nineveh will repent and that God will
forgive them. He is a man with a strong sense
of order and law, but without love. However, in
his attempt to escape he finds himself in the belly

---

[26] Chapter IV, Selfishness, Self-Love, and Self-Interest.

of a whale, symbolizing the state of isolation and imprisonment which his lack of love and solidarity has brought upon him. God saves him, and Jonah goes to Nineveh. He preaches to the inhabitants as God had told him, and the very thing he was afraid of happens. The men of Nineveh repent their sins, mend their ways, and God forgives them and decides not to destroy the city. Jonah is intensely angry and disappointed; he wanted "justice" to be done, not mercy. At last he finds some comfort by the shade of a tree which God had made to grow for him to protect him from the sun. But when God makes the tree wilt Jonah is depressed and angrily complains to God. God answers: "Thou hast had pity on the gourd for the which thou has not labored neither madest it grow; which came up in a night, and perished in a night. And should I not spare Nineveh, that great city, wherein are more than sixscore thousand people that cannot discern between their right hand and their left hand; and also much cattle?" God's answer to Jonah is to be understood symbolically. God explains to Jonah that the essence of love is to "labor" for something and "to make something grow," that love and labor are inseparable. One loves that for which one labors, and one labors for that which one loves.

The story of Jonah implies that love cannot be divorced from *responsibility*. Jonah does not feel responsible for the life of his brothers. He, like Cain, could ask, "Am I my brother's keeper?" Responsibility is not a duty imposed upon one from the outside, but is my response to a request which I feel to be my concern. Responsibility and response have the same root, *respondere* = "to answer"; to be responsible means to be ready to respond.

Motherly love is the most frequent and most readily understood instance of productive love; its very essence is care and responsibility. During the birth of the child the mother's body "labors" for the child and after birth her love consists in her effort to make the child grow. Motherly love does not depend on conditions which the child has to fulfill in order to be loved; it is unconditional, based only upon the child's request and the mother's response.[27] No wonder that motherly love has been a symbol of the highest form of love in art and religion. The Hebrew term indicating God's love for man and man's love for his neighbor is *rachamim*, the root of which is *rechem* = womb.

But not so evident is the connection of *care* and *responsibility* with individual love; it is believed that to fall in love is already the culmination of love, while actually it is the beginning and only an opportunity for the achievement of love. It is believed that love is the result of a mysterious quality by which two people are attracted to each other, an event which occurs without effort. Indeed, man's loneliness and his sexual desires make it easy to fall in love and there is nothing mysterious about it, but it is a gain which is as quickly lost as it has been achieved. One is not loved accidentally; one's own power to love produces love —just as being interested makes one interesting. People are concerned with the question of whether they are attractive while they forget that the essence of attractiveness is their own capacity to love. To love a person productively implies to care and to feel responsible for his life, not only

[27] Compare Aristotle on love: "But friendship seems to consist rather in loving than in being loved. It may be seen to be so by the delight which mothers have in loving; for mothers sometimes give their children to be brought up by others, and although they know them and love them, do not look for love in return, if it be impossible both to love and to be loved, but are content, as it seems, to see their children doing well, and to give them their love, even if the children in their ignorance do not render them any such service as is a mother's due."—Welldon translation, Book VIII, Chap. X.

for his physical existence but for the growth and development of all his human powers. To love productively is incompatible with being passive, with being an onlooker at the loved person's life; it implies labor and care and the responsibility for his growth.

In spite of the universalistic spirit of the monotheistic Western religions and of the progressive political concepts that are expressed in the idea "that all men are created equal," love for mankind has not become a common experience. Love for mankind is looked upon as an achievement which, at best, follows love for an individual or as an abstract concept to be realized only in the future. But love for man cannot be separated from the love for one individual. To love one person productively means to be related to his human core, to him as representing mankind. Love for one individual, in so far as it is divorced from love for man, can refer only to the superficial and to the accidental; of necessity it remains shallow. While it may be said that love for man differs from motherly love inasmuch as the child is helpless and our fellow men are not, it may also be said that even this difference exists only in relative terms. All men are in need of help and depend on one another. Human solidarity is the necessary condition for the unfolding of any one individual.

Care and responsibility are constituent elements of love, but without *respect* for and *knowledge* of the beloved person, love deteriorates into domination and possessiveness. Respect is not fear and awe; it denotes, in accordance with the root of the word (*respicere* = to look at), the ability to see a person as he is, to be aware of his individuality and uniqueness. To respect a person is not possible without knowing him; care and responsibility would be blind if they were not guided by the knowledge of the person's individuality.

A preliminary approach to the understanding of *productive thinking* may be made by examining the difference between reason and intelligence.

Intelligence is man's tool for attaining practical goals with the aim of discovering those aspects of things the knowledge of which is necessary for manipulating them. The goal itself or, what is the same, the premises on which "intelligent" thinking rests are not questioned, but are taken for granted and may or may not be rational in themselves. This particular quality of intelligence can be seen clearly in an extreme case, in that of the paranoid person. His premise, for instance, that all people are in conspiracy against him, is irrational and false, but his thought processes built upon this premise can in themselves show a remarkable amount of intelligence. In his attempt to prove his paranoid thesis he connects observations and makes logical constructions which are often so cogent that it is difficult to prove the irrationality of his premise. The application of mere intelligence to problems is, of course, not restricted to such pathological phenomena. Most of our thinking is necessarily concerned with the achievement of practical results, with the quantitative and "superficial" aspects of phenomena without inquiring into the validity of implied ends and premises and without attempting to understand the nature and quality of phenomena.

Reason involves a third dimension, that of depth, which reaches to the essence of things and processes. While reason is not divorced from the practical aims of life (and I shall show presently in what sense this is true), it is not a mere tool for immediate action. Its function is to know, to understand, to grasp, to relate oneself to things by comprehending them. It penetrates through the surface of things in order to discover their essence, their hidden relationships and deeper meanings, their "reason." It is, as it were, not

two-dimensional but "perspectivistic," to use
Nietzsche's term; i.e., it grasps all conceivable
perspectives and dimensions, not only the practi-
cally relevant ones. Being concerned with the
essence of things does not mean being concerned
with something "behind" things, but with the
essential, with the generic and the universal, with
the most general and pervasive traits of phenomena, freed from their superficial and accidental
(logically irrelevant) aspects.

We can now proceed to examine some more
specific characteristics of productive thinking. In
productive thinking the subject is not indifferent
to his object but is affected by and concerned with
it. The object is not experienced as something
dead and divorced from oneself and one's life,
as something about which one thinks only in a
self-isolated fashion; on the contrary, the subject
is intensely interested in his object, and the more
intimate this relation is, the more fruitful is his
thinking. It is this very relationship between him
and his object which stimulates his thinking in
the first place. To him a person or any phenomenon
becomes an object of thought because it is an
object of interest, relevant from the standpoint
of his individual life or that of human existence.
A beautiful illustration of this point is the story
of Buddha's discovery of the "fourfold truth."
Buddha saw a dead man, a sick man, and an old
man. He, a young man, was deeply affected by
the inescapable fate of man, and his reaction to
his observation was the stimulus for thinking
which resulted in his theory of the nature of life
and the ways of man's salvation. His reaction
was certainly not the only possible one. A modern
physician in the same situation might react by
starting to think of how to combat death, sickness,
and age, but his thinking would also be determined
by his total reaction to his object.

In the process of productive thinking the

thinker is motivated by his interest for the object; he is affected by it and reacts to it; he cares and responds. But productive thinking is also characterized by objectivity, by the respect the thinker has for his object, by his ability to see the object as it is and not as he wishes it to be. This polarity between objectivity and subjectivity is characteristic of productive thinking as it is of productiveness in general.

To be objective is possible only if we respect the things we observe; that is, if we are capable of seeing them in their uniqueness and their interconnectedness. This respect is not essentially different from the respect we discussed in connection with love; inasmuch as I want to understand something I must be able to see it as it exists according to its own nature; while this is true with regard to all objects of thought, it constitutes a special problem for the study of human nature.

Another aspect of objectivity must be present in productive thinking about living and nonliving objects: that of seeing the totality of a phenomenon. If the observer isolates one aspect of the object without seeing the whole, he will not properly understand even the one aspect he is studying. This point has been emphasized as the most important element in productive thinking by *Wertheimer*. "Productive processes," he writes, "are often of this nature: in the desire to get a real understanding, requestioning and investigation start. A certain region in the field becomes crucial, is focused; but it does not become isolated. A new, deeper structural view of the situation develops, involving changes in the functional meaning, the grouping, etc., of the items. Directed by what is required by the structure of a situation for a crucial region, one is led to a reasonable prediction, which—like the other parts of the structure—calls for verification, direct, or indirect. Two directions are involved: getting a whole consistent picture, and seeing what the structure of the whole requires for the parts."[28]

Objectivity requires not only seeing the object as it is but also seeing oneself as one is, i.e., being aware of the particular constellation in which one finds oneself as an observer related to the object of observation. Productive thinking, then, is determined by the nature of the object and the nature of the subject who relates himself to his object in the process of thinking. This twofold determination constitutes objectivity, in contrast to false subjectivity in which the thinking is not controlled by the object and thus degenerates into prejudice, wishful thinking, and fantasy. But objectivity is not, as it is often implied in a false idea of "scientific" objectivity, synonymous with detachment, with absence of interest and care. How can one penetrate the veiling surface of things to their causes and relationships if one does not have an interest that is vital and sufficiently impelling for so laborious a task? How could the aims of inquiry be formulated except by reference to the interests of man? *Objectivity does not mean detachment, it means respect;* that is, the ability not to distort and to falsify things, persons, and oneself. But does not the subjective factor in the observer, his interests, tend to distort his thinking for the sake of arriving at desired results? Is not the lack of personal interest the condition of scientific inquiry? The idea that lack of interest is a condition for recognizing the truth is fallacious.[29] There hardly has been any significant discovery or insight which has not been prompted by an interest of the thinker. In fact, without interests, thinking becomes sterile and pointless. What matters is

[28] Max Wertheimer, *Productive Thinking* (New York: Harper & Brothers, 1945), p. 167. Cf. also p. 192.

[29] Cf. K. Mannheim's discussion of this point in *Ideology and Utopia* (New York: Harcourt, Brace and Company, 1936).

not whether or not there is an interest, but *what kind* of interest there is and what its relation to the truth will be. All productive thinking is stimulated by the interest of the observer. It is never an interest per se which distorts ideas, but only those interests which are incompatible with the truth, with the discovery of the nature of the object under observation.

The statement that productiveness is an intrinsic human faculty contradicts the idea that man is lazy by nature and that he has to be forced to be active. This assumption is an old one. When Moses asked Pharaoh to let the Jewish people go so that they might "serve God in the desert," his answer was: "You are lazy, nothing but lazy." To Pharaoh, slave labor meant doing things; worshiping God was laziness. The same idea was adopted by all those who wanted to profit from the activity of others and had no use for productiveness, which they could not exploit.

Our own culture seems to offer evidence for the very opposite. For the last few centuries Western man has been obsessed by the idea of work, by the need for constant activity. He is almost incapable of being lazy for any length of time. This contrast, however, is only apparent. Laziness and compulsive activity are not opposites but are two symptoms of the disturbance of man's proper functioning. In the neurotic individual we often find the inability to work as his main symptom; in the so-called adjusted person, the inability to enjoy ease and repose. Compulsive activity is not the opposite of laziness but its complement; the opposite of both is productiveness.

The crippling of productive activity results in either inactivity or overactivity. Hunger and force can never be conditions of productive activity. On the contrary, freedom, economic security, and an organization of society in which work can be the meaningful expression of man's faculties are the factors conducive to the expression of man's natural tendency to make productive use of his powers. Productive activity is characterized by the rhythmic change of activity and repose. Productive work, love, and thought are possible only if a person can be, when necessary, quiet and alone with himself. To be able to listen to oneself is a prerequisite for the ability to listen to others; to be at home with oneself is the necessary condition for relating oneself to others.

(4) Orientations in the Process of Socialization

As pointed out in the beginning of this chapter, the process of living implies two kinds of relatedness to the outside world, that of assimilation and that of socialization. While the former has been discussed in detail in this chapter,[30] the latter has been dealt with at length in *Escape from Freedom* and therefore I will give here only a brief summary.

We can differentiate between the following kinds of interpersonal relatedness: *symbiotic relatedness, withdrawal-destructiveness, love.*

In the *symbiotic* relatedness the person is related to others but loses or never attains his independence; he avoids the danger of aloneness by becoming part of another person, either by being "swallowed" by that person or by "swallowing" him. The former is the root of what is clinically described as *masochism.* Masochism is the attempt to get rid of one's individual self, to escape from freedom, and to look for security by attaching oneself to another person. The forms which such dependency assume are manifold. It can be rationalized as sacrifice, duty, or love, especially when cultural patterns legitimatize this kind of

[30] Including love, which was treated together with all other manifestations of productiveness in order to give a fuller description of the nature of productiveness.

rationalization. Sometimes masochistic strivings
are blended with sexual impulses and pleasureful
(the masochistic perversion); often the masochistic strivings are so much in conflict with the parts
of the personality striving for independence and
freedom that they are experienced as painful and
tormenting.

The impulse to swallow others, the *sadistic*,
active form of symbiotic relatedness, appears in
all kinds of rationalizations, as love, overprotec-
tiveness, "justified" domination, "justified" ven-
geance, etc.; it also appears blended with sexual
impulses as sexual sadism. All forms of the sadistic
drive go back to the impulse to have complete
mastery over another person, to "swallow" him,
and to make him a helpless object of our will.
Complete domination over a powerless person is
the essence of active symbiotic relatedness. The
dominated person is perceived and treated as a
thing to be used and exploited, not as a human
being who is an end in himself. The more this
craving is blended with destructiveness, the more
cruel it is; but the benevolent domination which
often masquerades as "love" is an expression of
sadism too. While the benevolent sadist wants his
object to be rich, powerful, successful, there is one
thing he tries to prevent with all his power: that
his object become free and independent and thus
cease to be his.

Balzac in his *Lost Illusions* gives a striking
example of benevolent sadism. He describes the
relationship between young Lucien and the Bagno
prisoner who poses as an abbé. Shortly after he
makes the acquaintance of the young man who has
just tried to commit suicide, the abbé says: "I
have picked you up, I have given life to you, and
you belong to me as the creature belongs to the
creator, as—in the Orient's fairy tales—the Ifrit
belongs to the spirit, as the body belongs to the
soul. With powerful hands I will keep you straight

on the road to power; I promise you, nevertheless, a life of pleasure, of honors, of everlasting feasts. You will never lack money, you will sparkle, you will be brilliant; whereas I, stooped down in the filth of promoting, shall secure the brilliant edifice of your success. I love power for the sake of power! I shall always enjoy *your* pleasures although I shall have to renounce them. Shortly: I shall be one and the same person with you. . . . I will love my creature, I will mold him, will shape him to my services, in order to love him as a father loves his child. I shall drive at your side in your Tilbury, my dear boy, I shall delight in your successes with women. I shall say: I am this handsome young man."

While the symbiotic relationship is one of *closeness* to and intimacy with the object, although at the expense of freedom and integrity, a second kind of relatedness is one of *distance*, of *withdrawal* and *destructiveness*. The feeling of individual powerlessness can be overcome by withdrawal from others who are experienced as threats. To a certain extent withdrawal is part of the normal rhythm in any person's relatedness to the world, a necessity for contemplation, for study, for the reworking of materials, thoughts, attitudes. In the phenomenon here described, withdrawal becomes the main form of relatedness to others, a negative relatedness, as it were. Its emotional equivalent is the feeling of indifference toward others, often accompanied by a compensatory feeling of self-inflation. Withdrawal and indifference can, but need not, be conscious; as a matter of fact, in our culture they are mostly covered up by a superficial kind of interest and sociability.

Destructiveness is the *active* form of withdrawal; the impulse to destroy others follows from the fear of being destroyed by them. Since withdrawal and destructiveness are the passive and active forms of the same kind of relatedness, they are often blended, in varying proportions. Their difference, however, is greater than that between the active and the passive form of the symbiotic relatedness. Destructiveness results from a more intense and more complete blocking of productiveness than withdrawal. It is the perversion of the drive to live; it is the energy of *unlived life* transformed into energy for the destruction of life.

Love is the productive form of relatedness to others and to oneself. It implies responsibility, care, respect and knowledge, and the wish for the other person to grow and develop. It is the expression of intimacy between two human beings under the condition of the preservation of each other's integrity.

It follows from what has been set forth that there must be certain affinities between the various forms of orientations in the process of assimilation and socialization, respectively. The following chart gives a picture of the orientations which have been discussed and the affinities between them.[31]

ASSIMILATION	SOCIALIZATION

I. Nonproductive orientation

    a) Receiving ....Masochistic ⎫
        (Accepting)   (Loyalty) ⎪
                                 ⎬ symbiosis
    b) Exploiting ....Sadistic ⎪
        (Taking)   (Authority) ⎭

    c) Hoarding ....Destructive ⎫
        (Preserving) (Assertiveness) ⎪
                                  ⎬ withdrawal
    d) Marketing ....Indifferent ⎪
        (Exchanging)   (Fairness) ⎭

[31] The meaning of the concepts put in parentheses will be explained in the following section.

II. Productive orientation

Working ....Loving, Reasoning

Only a few words of comment seem to be needed. The receptive and exploitative attitude implies a different kind of interpersonal relationship from the hoarding one. Both the receptive and the exploitative attitudes result in a kind of intimacy and closeness to people from whom one expects to get the things needed either peacefully or aggressively. In the receptive attitude, the dominant relationship is a submissive, masochistic one: If I submit to the stronger person, he will give me all I need. The other person becomes the source of all good, and in the symbiotic relationship one receives all one needs from him. The exploitative attitude, on the other hand, implies usually a sadistic kind of relationship: If I take by force all I need from the other person, I must rule over him and make him the powerless object of my own domination.

In contrast to both these attitudes the hoarding kind of relatedness implies remoteness from other persons. It is based not on the expectation of getting things from an outside source of all good but on the expectation of having things by not consuming and by hoarding. Any intimacy with the outside world is a threat to this kind of autarchic security system. The hoarding character will tend to solve the problem of his relationship to others by attempting to withdraw or—if the outside world is felt to be too great a menace—to destroy.

The marketing orientation is also based on detachment from others, but in contrast to the hoarding orientation, the detachment has a friendly rather than a destructive connotation. The whole principle of the marketing orientation implies easy contact, superficial attachment, and

detachment from others only in a deeper emotional
sense.

(5) Blends of Various Orientations

In describing the different kinds of nonproductive orientations and the productive orientation,
I have dealt with these orientations as if they
were separate entities, clearly differentiated from
each other. For didactic purposes this kind of
treatment seemed to be necessary because we have
to understand the nature of each orientation before we can proceed to the understanding of their
blending. Yet, in reality, we always deal with
blends, for a character never represents one of the
nonproductive orientations or the productive
orientation exclusively.

Among the combinations of the various orientations we must differentiate between the blend of
the nonproductive orientations among themselves,
and that of the nonproductive with the productive
orientation. Some of the former have certain
affinities toward each other; for instance, the
receptive blends more frequently with the exploitative than with the hoarding orientation. The
receptive and exploitative orientations have in
common the closeness toward the object, in contrast to the remoteness of the person from the
object, in the hoarding orientation. However, even
the orientations with lesser affinity are frequently
blended. If one wants to characterize a person,
one will usually have to do so in terms of his
dominant orientation.

The blending between the nonproductive and
productive orientation needs a more thorough discussion. There is no person whose orientation is
entirely productive, and no one who is completely
lacking in productiveness. But the respective
weight of the productive and the nonproductive
orientation in each person's character structure

varies and determines the *quality* of the non-productive orientations. In the foregoing description of the nonproductive orientations it was assumed that they were *dominant* in a character structure. We must now supplement the earlier description by considering the qualities of the nonproductive orientations in a character structure in which the *productive* orientation is *dominant*. Here the nonproductive orientations do not have the negative meaning they have when they are dominant but have a different and constructive quality. In fact, the nonproductive orientations as they have been described may be considered as distortions of orientations which in themselves are a normal and necessary part of living. Every human being, in order to survive, must be able to *accept* things from others, to *take* things, to *save*, and to *exchange*. He must also be able to *follow authority*, to *guide others*, to be *alone*, and to *assert* himself. Only if his way of acquiring things and relating himself to others is essentially nonproductive does the ability to accept, to take, to save, or to exchange turn into the craving to receive, to exploit, to hoard, or to market as the dominant ways of acquisition. The nonproductive forms of social relatedness in a predominantly productive person—loyalty, authority, fairness, assertiveness—turn into submission, domination, withdrawal, destructiveness in a predominantly nonproductive person. Any of the nonproductive orientations has, therefore, a positive and a negative aspect, according to the degree of productiveness in the total character structure. The following list of the positive and negative aspects of various orientations may serve as an illustration for this principle.

RECEPTIVE ORIENTATION (ACCEPTING)

Positive Aspect	*Negative Aspect*
accepting	passive, without initiative
responsive	opinionless, characterless
devoted	submissive
modest	without pride
charming	parasitical
adaptable	unprincipled
socially adjusted	servile, without self-confidence
idealistic	unrealistic
sensitive	cowardly
polite	spineless
optimistic	wishful thinking
trusting	gullible
tender	sentimental

EXPLOITATIVE ORIENTATION (TAKING)

Positive Aspect	*Negative Aspect*
active	exploitative
able to take initiative	aggressive
able to make claims	egocentric
proud	conceited
impulsive	rash
self-confident	arrogant
captivating	seducing

HOARDING ORIENTATION (PRESERVING)

Positive Aspect	*Negative Aspect*
practical	unimaginative
economical	stingy
careful	suspicious
reserved	cold
patient	lethargic
cautious	anxious
steadfast, tenacious	stubborn
imperturbable	indolent
composed under stress	inert
orderly	pedantic
methodical	obsessional
loyal	possessive

MARKETING ORIENTATION (EXCHANGING)

Positive Aspect	*Negative Aspect*
purposeful	opportunistic
able to change	inconsistent
youthful	childish
forward-looking	without a future or a past
open-minded	without principle and values
social	unable to be alone
experimenting	aimless
undogmatic	relativistic
efficient	overactive
curious	tactless
intelligent	intellectualistic
adaptable	undiscriminating
tolerant	indifferent
witty	silly
generous	wasteful

The positive and negative aspects are not two separate classes of syndromes. Each of these traits can be described as a point in a continuum which is determined by *the degree of the productive orientation which prevails;* rational systematic orderliness, for instance, may be found when productiveness is high, while, with decreasing productiveness, it degenerates more and more into irrational, pedantic compulsive "orderliness" which actually defeats its own purpose. The same holds true of the change from youthfulness to childishness, or of the change from being proud to being conceited. In considering only the basic orientations we see the staggering amount of variability in each person brought about by the fact that

1) the nonproductive orientations are blended in different ways with regard to the respective weight of each of them;

2) each changes in quality according to the amount of productiveness present;

3) the different orientations may operate in

different strength in the material, emotional, or intellectual spheres of activity, respectively.

If we add to the picture of personality the different temperaments and gifts, we can easily recognize that the configuration of these basic elements makes for an endless number of variations in personality.

CHAPTER IV

PROBLEMS OF HUMANISTIC ETHICS

The most obvious argument against the principle of humanistic ethics—that virtue is the same as the pursuit of man's obligations toward himself, and vice the same as self-mutilation—is that we make egotism or selfishness the norm of human conduct when actually the aim of ethics should be its defeat, and, further, that we overlook man's innate evilness which can be curbed only by his fear of sanctions and awe of authorities. Or, if man is not innately bad, the argument may run, is he not constantly seeking for pleasure, and is not pleasure itself against, or at least indifferent to, the principles of ethics? Is not conscience the only effective agent in man causing him to act virtuously, and has not conscience lost its place in humanistic ethics? There seems to be no place for faith either; yet is not faith a necessary basis of ethical behavior?

These questions imply certain assumptions about human nature and become a challenge to any psychologist who is concerned with the achievement of man's happiness and growth, and consequently with moral norms conducive to this aim. In this chapter I shall attempt to deal with these problems in the light of the psychoanalytic data the theoretical foundation for which was laid in the chapter entitled Human Nature and Character.

1. Selfishness, Self-Love, and Self-Interest[1]

> Thou shalt love thy neighbour as thyself.
> —Bible

Modern culture is pervaded by a tabu on selfishness. We are taught that to be selfish is sinful and that to love others is virtuous. To be sure, this doctrine is in flagrant contradiction to the practice of modern society, which holds the doctrine that the most powerful and legitimate drive in man is selfishness and that by following this imperative drive the individual makes his best contribution to the common good. But the doctrine which declares selfishness to be the arch evil and love for others to be the greatest virtue is still powerful. Selfishness is used here almost synonymously with self-love. The alternative is to love others, which is a virtue, or to love oneself, which is a sin.

This principle has found its classic expression in Calvin's theology, according to which man is essentially evil and powerless. Man can achieve absolutely nothing that is good on the basis of his own strength or merit. "We are not our own," says Calvin. "Therefore neither our reason nor our will should predominate in our deliberations and actions. We are not our own; therefore let us not propose it as our end to seek what may be expedient for us according to the flesh. We are not our own; therefore, let us, as far as possible, forget ourselves and all things that are ours. On the contrary, we are God's; for Him, therefore, let us live and die. For, as it is the most devastating pestilence which ruins people if they obey themselves, it is the only haven of salvation not

[1] Cf. Erich Fromm, "Selfishness and Self-Love," *Psychiatry* (November, 1939). The following discussion of selfishness and self-love is a partial repetition of the earlier paper.

to know or to want anything by oneself but to be guided by God Who walks before us."[2] Man should have not only the conviction of his absolute nothingness but he should do everything to humiliate himself. "For I do not call it humility if you suppose that we have anything left . . . . we cannot think of ourselves as we ought to think without utterly despising everything that may be supposed an excellence in us. This humility is unfeigned submission of a mind overwhelmed with a weighty sense of its own misery and poverty; for such is the uniform description of it in the word of God."[3]

This emphasis on the nothingness and wickedness of the individual implies that there is nothing he should like and respect about himself. The doctrine is rooted in self-contempt and self-hatred. Calvin makes this point very clear: he speaks of self-love as "a pest."[4] If the individual finds something "on the strength of which he finds pleasure in himself," he betrays this sinful self-love. This fondness for himself will make him sit in judgment over others and despise them. Therefore, to be fond of oneself or to like anything in oneself is one of the greatest sins. It is supposed to exclude love for others[5]

[2] Johannes Calvin, *Institutes of the Christian Religion*, trans. by John Allen (Philadelphia: Presbyterian Board of Christian Education, 1928), in particular Book III, Chap. 7, p. 619. From "For, as it is . . . ." the translation is mine from the Latin original (Johannes Calvini. *Institutio Christianae Religionis. Editionem curavit*, A. Tholuk, Berolini, 1935, par. 1, p. 445).

[3] *Ibid.*, Chap. 12, par. 6, p. 681.

[4] *Ibid.*, Chap. 7, par. 4, p. 622.

[5] It should be noted, however, that even love for one's neighbor, while it is one of the fundamental doctrines of the New Testament, has not been given a corresponding weight by Calvin. In blatant contradiction to the New Testament, Calvin says: "For what the schoolmen advance concerning the priority of charity to faith and hope, is a mere reverie of a distempered imagination . . . ."—Chap. 24, par. 1, p. 531.

and to be identical with selfishness.[6]

The view of man held by Calvin and Luther has been of tremendous influence on the development of modern Western society. They laid the foundations for an attitude in which man's own happiness was not considered to be the aim of life but where he became a means, an adjunct, to ends beyond him, of an all-powerful God, or of the not less powerful secularized authorities and norms, the state, business, success. Kant, who, with regard to the idea that man should be an end in himself and never a means only, was perhaps the most influential ethical thinker of the Enlightenment period, nevertheless had the same condemnation for self-love. According to him, it is a virtue to want happiness for others, but to want one's own happiness is ethically indifferent, since it is something for which the nature of man is striving, and since a natural striving cannot have a positive ethical value.[7] Kant admits that one must not give up one's claims to happiness; under certain circumstances it may even be a duty to be concerned with it, partly because health, wealth, and the like may be means necessary for the fulfillment of one's duty, partly because the lack of happiness—poverty—can prevent one from fulfilling his duty.[8] But love for oneself, striving for one's own happiness, can never be a *virtue*. As an ethical principle, the striving for one's own happiness "is the most objectionable one, not merely

[6] Despite Luther's emphasis on the spiritual freedom of the individual, his theology, different as it is in many ways from Calvin's, is pervaded by the same conviction of man's basic powerlessness and nothingness.

[7] Compare Immanuel Kant, *Kant's Critique of Practical Reason and Other Works on the Theory of Ethics*, trans. by Thomas Kingsmill Abbott (New York: Longmans, Green & Co., 1909), Part I, Book I, Chap. I, par. VIII, Remark II, p. 126.

[8] *Ibid.*, in particular Part I, Book I, Chap. III, p. 186.

because it is false . . . . but because the springs
it provides for morality are such as rather to
undermine it and destroy its sublimity . . . ."[9]

Kant differentiates egotism, self-love, *philautia*
—a benevolence for oneself—and arrogance, the
pleasure in oneself. But even "rational self-love"
must be restricted by ethical principles, the pleasure in oneself must be battered down, and the
individual must come to feel humiliated in comparing himself with the sanctity of moral laws.[10]
The individual should find supreme happiness in
the fulfillment of his duty. The realization of the
moral principle—and, therefore, of the individual's happiness—is only possible in the general
whole, the nation, the state. But "the welfare of
the state"—and *salus rei publicae suprema lex
est*—is not identical with the welfare of the citi-
zens and their happiness.[11]

In spite of the fact that Kant shows a greater
respect for the integrity of the individual than did
Calvin or Luther, he denies the individual's right
to rebel even under the most tyrannical govern-
ment; the rebel must be punished with no less
than death if he threatens the sovereign.[12] Kant
emphasizes the native propensity for evil in the
nature of man,[13] for the suppression of which the
moral law, the categorical imperative, is essential
lest man should become a beast and human society
end in wild anarchy.

[9] *Loc. cit.*, *Fundamental Principles of the Metaphysics
of Morals;* second section, p. 61.

[10] *Loc. cit.*, Part I, Book I, Ch. III, p. 165.

[11] Immanuel Kant, *Immanuel Kant's Werke* (Berlin:
Cassierer), in particular "Der Rechtslehre Zweiter Teil"
I. Abschnitt, par. 49, p. 124. I translate from the German
text, since this part is omitted in the English translation
of *The Metaphysics of Ethics* by I. W. Semple (Edinburgh: 1871).

[12] *Ibid.*, p. 126.

[13] Compare Immanuel Kant, *Religion within the Limits of
Reason Alone*, trans. by T. M. Greene and H. H. Hudson
(Chicago: Open Court, 1934), Book I.

In the philosophy of the Enlightenment period the individual's claims to happiness have been emphasized much more strongly by others than by Kant, for instance, by Helvetius. This trend in modern philosophy has found its most radical expression in Stirner and Nietzsche.[14] But while they take the opposite position to that of Calvin and Kant with regard to the value of selfishness, they agree with them in the assumption that love for others and love for oneself are alternatives. They denounce love for others as weakness and self-sacrifice and postulate egotism, selfishness, and self-love—they too confuse the issue by not clearly differentiating between these last—as virtue. Thus Stirner says: "Here, egoism, selfishness must decide, not the principle of love, not love motives like mercy, gentleness, good-nature, or even justice and equity—for *iustitia* too is a phenomenon of love, a product of love; love knows only sacrifice and demands self-sacrifice."[15]

The kind of love denounced by Stirner is the masochistic dependence by which the individual makes himself a means for achieving the purposes of somebody or something outside himself. Opposing this concept of love, he did not avoid a formulation, which, highly polemical, overstates the point. The positive principle with which Stirner was concerned[16] was opposed to an attitude which

[14] In order not to make this chapter too long I discuss only the modern philosophical development. The student of philosophy will know that Aristotle's and Spinoza's ethics consider self-love a virtue, not a vice, in striking contrast to Calvin's standpoint.

[15] Max Stirner, *The Ego and His Own*, trans. by S. T. Byington (London: A. C. Fifield, 1912), p. 339.

[16] One of his positive formulations, for example, is: "But how does one use life? In using it up like the candle one burns. . . . Enjoyment of life is using life up." F. Engels has clearly seen the one-sidedness of Stirner's formulations and has attempted to overcome the false alternative between love for oneself and love for others. In a letter to Marx in which he discusses Stirner's book, Engels writes:

had been that of Christian theology for centuries
—and which was vivid in the German idealism
prevalent in his time; namely, to bend the individual so that he submits to, and finds his center
in, a power and a principle outside himself. Stirner was not a philosopher of the stature of Kant
or Hegel, but he had the courage to rebel radically
against that side of idealistic philosophy which
negated the concrete individual and thus helped
the absolute state to retain its oppressive power
over him.

In spite of many differences between *Nietzsche*
and *Stirner*, their ideas in this respect are very
much the same. Nietzsche too denounces love and
altruism as expressions of weakness and self-negation. For Nietzsche, the quest for love is
typical of slaves unable to fight for what they
want and who therefore try to get it through love.
Altruism and love for mankind thus have become
a sign of degeneration.[17] For Nietzsche it is the
essence of a good and healthy aristocracy that it
is ready to sacrifice countless people for its interests without having a guilty conscience. Society
should be a "foundation and scaffolding by means
of which a select class of beings may be able to
elevate themselves to their higher duties, and in
general to a higher existence."[18] Many quotations
could be added to document this spirit of contempt
and egotism. These ideas have often been under-

"If, however, the concrete and real individual is the true
basis for our 'human' man, it is self-evident that egotism—
of course not only Stirner's egotism of reason, but also the
egotism of the heart—is the basis for our love of man."—
Marx-Engels Gesamtausgabe (Berlin: Marx-Engels Verlag, 1929), p. 6.

[17] Friedrich Nietzsche, *The Will to Power*, trans. by
Anthony M. Ludovici (Edinburgh and London: T. N.
Foulis, 1910), stanzas 246, 326, 369, 373, and 728.

[18] Friedrich Nietzsche, *Beyond Good and Evil*, trans. by
Helen Zimmer (New York: The Macmillan Company,
1907), stanza 258.

stood as *the* philosophy of Nietzsche. However, they do not represent the true core of his philosophy.[19]

There are various reasons why Nietzsche expressed himself in the sense noted above. First of all, as with Stirner, his philosophy is a reaction —a rebellion—against the philosophical tradition of subordinating the empirical individual to powers and principles outside himself. His tendency to overstatement shows this reactive quality. Second, there were, in Nietzsche's personality, feelings of insecurity and anxiety that made him emphasize the "strong man" as a reaction formation. Finally, Nietzsche was impressed by the theory of evolution and its emphasis on the "survival of the fittest." This interpretation does not alter the fact that Nietzsche believed that there is a contradiction between love for others and love for oneself; yet his views contain the nucleus from which this false dichotomy can be overcome. The "love" which he attacks is rooted not in one's own strength, but in one's own weakness. "Your neighbor-love is your bad love of yourselves. Ye flee unto your neighbor from yourselves and would fain make a virtue thereof! But I fathom your 'unselfishness.'" He states explicitly, "You cannot stand yourselves and you do not love yourselves sufficiently."[20] For Nietzsche the individual has "an enormously great significance."[21] The "strong" individual is the one who has "true kindness, nobility, greatness of soul, which does not give in order to take, which does not want to excel by being kind;—'waste' as type of true kindness, wealth of the person as a premise."[22] He expresses

---

[19] Cf. G. A. Morgan, *What Nietzsche Means* (Cambridge: Harvard University Press, 1943).

[20] Friedrich Nietzsche, *Thus Spake Zarathustra*, trans. by Thomas Common (New York: Modern Library), p. 75.

[21] *The Will to Power*, stanza 785.

[22] *Ibid.*, stanza 935.

the same thought also in *Thus Spake Zarathustra:* "The one goeth to his neighbor because he
seeketh himself, and the other because he would
fain lose himself."[23]

The essence of this view is this: Love is a phenomenon of abundance; its premise is the
strength of the individual who can give. Love is
affirmation and productiveness, "It seeketh to
create what is loved!"[24] To love another person
is only a virtue if it springs from this inner
strength, but it is a vice if it is the expression of
the basic inability to be oneself.[25] However, the
fact remains that Nietzsche left the problem of
the relationship between self-love and love for
others as an unsolved antinomy.

The doctrine that selfishness is the arch-evil and
that to love oneself excludes loving others is by no
means restricted to theology and philosophy, but
it became one of the stock ideas promulgated in
home, school, motion pictures, books; indeed in
all instruments of social suggestion as well. "Don't
be selfish" is a sentence which has been impressed
upon millions of children, generation after generation. Its meaning is somewhat vague. Most people
would say that it means not to be egotistical, in-
considerate, without any concern for others. Actually, it generally means more than that. Not to
be selfish implies not to do what one wishes, to
give up one's own wishes for the sake of those in
authority. "Don't be selfish," in the last analysis,
has the same ambiguity that it has in Calvinism.
Aside from its obvious implication, it means,
"don't love yourself," "don't be yourself," but sub-

[23] *Thus Spake Zarathustra*, p. 76.

[24] *Ibid.*, p. 102.

[25] See Friedrich Nietzsche, *The Twilight of Idols*, trans.
by A. M. Ludovici (Edinburgh: T. N. Foulis, 1911), stanza
35; *Ecce Homo*, trans. by A. M. Ludovici (New York:
The Macmillan Company, 1911), stanza 2; *Nachlass,
Neitzsches Werke* (Leipzig: A. Kroener), pp. 63–64.

mit yourself to something more important than yourself, to an outside power or its internalization, "duty." "Don't be selfish" becomes one of the most powerful ideological tools in suppressing spontaneity and the free development of personality. Under the pressure of this slogan one is asked for every sacrifice and for complete submission: only those acts are "unselfish" which do not serve the individual but somebody or something outside himself.

This picture, we must repeat, is in a certain sense one-sided. For besides the doctrine that one should not be selfish, the opposite is also propagandized in modern society: keep your own advantage in mind, act according to what is best for you; by so doing you will also be acting for the greatest advantage of all others. As a matter of fact, the idea that egotism is the basis of the general welfare is the principle on which competitive society has been built. It is puzzling that two such seemingly contradictory principles could be taught side by side in one culture; of the fact, however, there is no doubt. One result of this contradiction is confusion in the individual. Torn between the two doctrines, he is seriously blocked in the process of integrating his personality. This confusion is one of the most significant sources of the bewilderment and helplessness of modern man.[26]

The doctrine that love for oneself is identical with "selfishness" and an alternative to love for others has pervaded theology, philosophy, and popular thought; the same doctrine has been rationalized in scientific language in *Freud's* theory of narcissism. Freud's concept presupposes

[26] This point has been emphasized by Karen Horney, *The Neurotic Personality of Our Time* (New York: W. W. Norton & Company, 1937), and by Robert S. Lynd, *Knowledge for What?* (Princeton: Princeton University Press, 1939).

a fixed amount of libido. In the infant, all of the libido has the child's own person as its objective, the stage of "primary narcissism," as Freud calls it. During the individual's development, the libido is shifting from one's own person toward other objects. If a person is blocked in his "object-relationships," the libido is withdrawn from the objects and returned to his own person; this is called "secondary narcissism." According to Freud, the more love I turn toward the outside world the less love is left for myself, and vice versa. He thus describes the phenomenon of love as an impoverishment of one's self-love because all libido is turned to an object outside oneself.

These questions arise: Does psychological observation support the thesis that there is a basic contradiction and a state of alternation between love for oneself and love for others? Is love for oneself the same phenomenon as selfishness, or are they opposites? Furthermore, is the selfishness of modern man really a *concern for himself* as an individual, with all his intellectual, emotional, and sensual potentialities? Has "he" not become an appendage of his socioeconomic role? *Is his selfishness identical with self-love or is it not caused by the very lack of it?*

Before we start the discussion of the psychological aspect of selfishness and self-love, the logical fallacy in the notion that love for others and love for oneself are mutually exclusive should be stressed. If it is a virtue to love my neighbor as a human being, it must be a virtue—and not a vice—to love myself since I am a human being too. There is no concept of man in which I myself am not included. A doctrine which proclaims such an exclusion proves itself to be intrinsically contradictory. The idea expressed in the Biblical "Love thy neighbor as thyself!" implies that respect for one's own integrity and uniqueness, love for and understanding of one's own self, can not be separated from respect for and love and understanding of another individual. The love for my own self is inseparably connected with the love for any other self.

We have come now to the basic psychological premises on which the conclusions of our argument are built. Generally, these premises are as follows: not only others, but we ourselves are the "object" of our feelings and attitudes; the attitudes toward others and toward ourselves, far from being contradictory, are basically *conjunctive*. With regard to the problem under discussion this means: Love of others and love of ourselves are not alternatives. On the contrary, an attitude of love toward themselves will be found in all those who are capable of loving others. *Love,* in principle, *is indivisible as far as the connection between "objects" and one's own self is concerned.* Genuine love is an expression of productiveness and implies care, respect, responsibility, and knowledge. It is not an "affect" in the sense of being affected by somebody, but an active striving for the growth and happiness of the loved person, rooted in one's own capacity to love.

To love is an expression of one's power to love, and to love somebody is the actualization and concentration of this power with regard to one person. It is not true, as the idea of romantic love would have it, that there is only *the* one person in the world whom one could love and that it is the great chance of one's life to find that one person. Nor is it true, if that person be found that love for him (or her) results in a withdrawal of love from others. Love which can only be experienced with regard to one person demonstrates by this very fact that it is not love, but a symbiotic attachment. The basic affirmation contained in love is directed toward the beloved person as an incarnation of essentially human qualities. Love of one person implies love of man as such. The kind of "division of labor," as William James calls it, by which one loves one's family but is without feeling for the "stranger," is a sign of a basic inability to love. Love of man is not, as is frequently supposed, an abstraction coming after the love for a specific person, but it is its premise, although, genetically, it is acquired in loving specific individuals.

From this it follows that my own self, in principle, must be as much an object of my love as another person. *The affirmation of one's own life, happiness, growth, freedom, is rooted in one's capacity to love,* i.e., in care, respect, responsibility, and knowledge. If an individual is able to love productively, he loves himself too; if he can love *only* others, he can not love at all.

Granted that love for oneself and for others in principle is conjunctive, how do we explain selfishness, which obviously excludes any genuine concern for others? The *selfish* person is interested only in himself, wants everything for himself, feels no pleasure in giving, but only in taking. The world outside is looked at only from the standpoint of what he can get out of it; he lacks interest in the needs of others, and respect for their dignity and integrity. He can see nothing but himself; he judges everyone and everything from its usefulness to him; he is basically unable to love. Does not this prove that concern for others and concern for oneself are unavoidable alternatives? This would be so if selfishness and self-love were identical. But that assumption is the very fallacy which has led to so many mistaken conclusions concerning our problem. *Selfishness and self-love, far from being identical, are actually opposites*. The selfish person does not love himself too much but too little; in fact he hates himself. This lack of fondness and care for himself, which is only one expression of his lack of productiveness, leaves him empty and frustrated. He is necessarily un-

happy and anxiously concerned to snatch from
life the satisfactions which he blocks himself
from attaining. He seems to care too much for
himself but actually he only makes an unsuccessful attempt to cover up and compensate for his
failure to care for his real self. Freud holds that
the selfish person is narcissistic, as if he had withdrawn his love from others and turned it toward
his own person. *It is true that selfish persons are
incapable of loving others, but they are not capable of loving themselves either.*

It is easier to understand selfishness by comparing it with greedy concern for others, as we
find it, for instance, in an oversolicitous, dominating mother. While she consciously believes that she
is particularly fond of her child, she has actually a
deeply repressed hostility toward the object of
her concern. She is overconcerned not because she
loves the child too much, but because she has to
compensate for her lack of capacity to love him
at all.

This theory of the nature of selfishness is borne
out by psychoanalytic experience with neurotic
"unselfishness," a symptom of neurosis observed
in not a few people who usually are troubled not
by this symptom but by others connected with it,
like depression, tiredness, inability to work, failure in love relationships, and so on. Not only is
unselfishness not felt as a "symptom"; it is often
the one redeeming character trait on which such
people pride themselves. The "unselfish" person
"does not want anything for himself"; he "lives
only for others," is proud that he does not consider
himself important. He is puzzled to find that in
spite of his unselfishness he is unhappy, and that
his relationships to those closest to him are unsatisfactory. He wants to have what he considers
are his symptoms removed—but not his unselfishness. Analytic work shows that his unselfishness
is not something apart from his other symptoms

but one of them; in fact often the most important one; that he is paralyzed in his capacity to love or to enjoy anything; that he is pervaded by hostility against life and that behind the façade of unselfishness a subtle but not less intense self-centeredness is hidden. This person can be cured only if his unselfishness too is interpreted as a symptom along with the others so that his lack of productiveness, which is at the root of both his unselfishness *and* his other troubles, can be corrected.

The nature of unselfishness becomes particularly apparent in its effect on others and most frequently, in our culture, in the effect the "unselfish" mother has on her children. She believes that by her unselfishness her children will experience what it means to be loved and to learn, in turn, what it means to love. The effect of her unselfishness, however, does not at all correspond to her expectations. The children do not show the happiness of persons who are convinced that they are loved; they are anxious, tense, afraid of the mother's disapproval and anxious to live up to her expectations. Usually, they are affected by their mother's hidden hostility against life, which they sense rather than recognize, and eventually become imbued with it themselves. Altogether, the effect of the "unselfish" mother is not too different from that of the selfish one; indeed, it is often worse because the mother's unselfishness prevents the children from criticizing her. They are put under the obligation not to disappoint her; they are taught, under the mask of virtue, dislike for life. If one has a chance to study the effect of a mother with genuine self-love, one can see that there is nothing more conducive to giving a child the experience of what love, joy, and happiness are than being loved by a mother who loves herself.

Having analyzed selfishness and self-love we can now proceed to discuss the concept of *self-*

interest, which has become one of the key symbols in modern society. It is even more ambiguous than selfishness or self-love, and this ambiguity can be fully understood only by taking into account the historical development of the concept of self-interest. The problem is what is considered to constitute self-interest and how it can be determined.

There are two fundamentally different approaches to this problem. One is the objectivistic approach most clearly formulated by Spinoza. To him self-interest or the interest "to seek one's profit" is identical with virtue. "The more," he says, "each person strives and is able *to seek his profit,* that is to say, to preserve his being, the more virtue does he possess; on the other hand, in so far as each person neglects his own profit he is impotent."[27] According to this view, the interest of man is to preserve his existence, which is the same as realizing his inherent potentialities. This concept of self-interest is objectivistic inasmuch as "interest" is not conceived in terms of the subjective feeling of what one's interest is but in terms of what the nature of man is, objectively. Man has only one real interest and that is the full development of his potentialities, of himself as a human being. Just as one has to know another person and his real needs in order to love him, one has to know one's own self in order to understand what the interests of this self are and how they can be served. It follows that man can deceive himself about his real self-interest if he is ignorant of his self and its real needs and that the science of man is the basis for determining what constitutes man's self-interest.

In the last three hundred years the concept of self-interest has increasingly been narrowed until it has assumed almost the opposite meaning which

[27] Spinoza, *Ethics,* IV, Prop. 20.

it has in Spinoza's thinking. It has become identical with selfishness, with interest in material gains, power, and success; and instead of its being synonymous with virtue, its conquest has become an ethical commandment.

This deterioration was made possible by the change from the objectivistic into the erroneously subjectivistic approach to self-interest. Self-interest was no longer to be determined by the nature of man and his needs; correspondingly, the notion that one could be mistaken about it was relinquished and replaced by the idea that what a person *felt* represented the interest of his self was necessarily his true self-interest.

The modern concept of self-interest is a strange blend of two contradictory concepts: that of Calvin and Luther on the one hand, and on the other, that of the progressive thinkers since Spinoza. Calvin and Luther had taught that man must suppress his self-interest and consider himself only an instrument for God's purposes. Progressive thinkers, on the contrary, have taught that man ought to be only an end for himself and not a means for any purpose transcending him. What happened was that man has accepted the contents of the Calvinistic doctrine while rejecting its religious formulation. He has made himself an instrument, not of God's will but of the economic machine or the state. He has accepted the role of a tool, not for God but for industrial progress; he has worked and amassed money but essentially not for the pleasure of spending it and of enjoying life but in order to save, to invest, to be successful. Monastic asceticism has been, as Max Weber has pointed out, replaced by an *inner-worldly asceticism* where personal happiness and enjoyment are no longer the real aims of life. But this attitude was increasingly divorced from the one expressed in Calvin's concept and blended with that expressed in the progressive concept of self-interest, which taught that man had the right—and the obligation—to make the pursuit of his self-interest the supreme norm of life. The result is that modern man *lives* according to the principles of self-denial and *thinks* in terms of self-interest. He believes that he is acting in behalf of *his* interest when actually his paramount concern is money and success; he deceives himself about the fact that his most important human potentialities remain unfulfilled and that he loses himself in the process of seeking what is supposed to be best for him.

The deterioration of the meaning of the concept of self-interest is closely related to the change in the concept of self. In the Middle Ages man felt himself to be an intrinsic part of the social and religious community in reference to which he conceived his own self when he as an individual had not yet fully emerged from his group. Since the beginning of the modern era, when man as an individual was faced with the task of experiencing himself as an independent entity, his own identity became a problem. In the eighteenth and nineteenth centuries the concept of self was narrowed down increasingly; the self was felt to be constituted by the property one had. The formula for this concept of self was no longer "I am what I think" but "I am what I have," "what I possess."[28]

---

[28] William James expressed this concept very clearly. "To have," he says, "a self that I can care for, Nature must first present me with some object interesting enough to make me instinctively wish to appropriate it for its own sake. . . . My own body and what ministers to its needs are thus the primitive object, instinctively determined, of my egoistic interests. Other objects may become interesting derivatively, through association with any of these things, either as means or as habitual concomitants; and so, in a thousand ways, the primitive sphere of the egoistic emotions may enlarge and change its boundaries. This sort of interest is really the meaning of the word *mine*. Whatever has it, is, *eo ipso*, a part of me!"—*Principles of Psychology* (New York: Henry Holt and Company, 2 vols.,

In the last few generations, under the growing influence of the market, the concept of self has shifted from meaning "I am what I possess" to meaning "I am as you desire me."[29] Man, living in a market economy, feels himself to be a commodity. He is divorced from himself, as the seller of a commodity is divorced from what he wants to sell. To be sure, he is interested in himself, immensely interested in his success on the market, but "he" is the manager, the employer, the seller—and the commodity. His self-interest turns out to be the interest of "him" as the subject who employs "himself" as the commodity which should obtain the optimal price on the personality market.

The "fallacy of self-interest" in modern man has never been described better than by Ibsen in *Peer Gynt.* Peer Gynt believes that his whole life is devoted to the attainment of the interests of his *self.* He describes this self as:

"The Gyntian Self!
—An army, that, of wishes, appetites, desires!
The Gyntian Self!
It is a sea of fancies, claims and aspirations;

1896), I, 319, 324. Elsewhere James writes: "It is clear that between what a man calls *me* and what he simply calls *mine,* the line is difficult to draw. We feel and act about certain things that are ours very much as we feel and act about ourselves. Our fame, our children, the work of our hands, may be as dear to us as our bodies are, and arouse the same feelings and the same acts of reprisal if attacked. . . . In its widest possible sense, however, a man's Self is the sum-total of all that he can call his, not only his body, and his psychic powers, but his clothes and his house, his wife and children, his ancestors and friends, his reputation and works, his land and horses and yacht and bank account. All these things give him the same emotions. If they wax or prosper, he feels triumphant, if they dwindle and die away, he feels cast down—not necessarily in the same degree for each thing, but in much the same way for all."—*Ibid.,* I, 291–292.

²⁹ Pirandello in his plays has expressed this concept of self and the self-doubt resulting from it.

In fact, it's all that swells within my breast
And makes it come about that I am I and live as
such."[30]

At the end of his life he recognizes that he had
deceived himself; that while following the principle of "self-interest" he had failed to recognize
what the interests of his real self were, and had
lost the very self he sought to preserve. He is told
that he never had been himself and that therefore
he is to be thrown back into the melting pot to
be dealt with as raw material. He discovers that
he has lived according to the Troll principle: "To
thyself be enough"—which is the opposite of the
human principle: "To thyself be true." He is
seized by the horror of nothingness to which he,
who has no self, can not help succumbing when the
props of pseudo self, success, and possessions are
taken away or seriously questioned. He is forced
to recognize that in trying to gain all the wealth
of the world, in relentlessly pursuing what seemed
to be his interest, he had lost his soul—or, as I
would rather say, his self.

The deteriorated meaning of the concept of self-
interest which pervades modern society has given
rise to attacks on democracy from the various
types of totalitarian ideologies. These claim that
capitalism is *morally* wrong because it is governed
by the principle of selfishness, and commend the
moral superiority of their own systems by pointing to their principle of the unselfish subordination
of the individual to the "higher" purposes of the
state, the "race," or the "socialist fatherland."
They impress not a few with this criticism because
many people feel that there is no happiness in the
pursuit of selfish interest, and are imbued with a
striving, vague though it may be, for a greater
solidarity and mutual responsibility among men.

[30] *Loc. cit.*, Act V, Scene I.

We need not waste much time arguing against the totalitarian claims. In the first place, they are insincere since they only disguise the extreme selfishness of an "elite" that wishes to conquer and retain power over the majority of the population. Their ideology of unselfishness has the purpose of deceiving those subject to the control of the elite and of facilitating their exploitation and manipulation. Furthermore, the totalitarian ideologies confuse the issue by making it appear that they represent the principle of unselfishness when they apply to the state as a whole the principle of ruthless pursuit of selfishness. Each citizen ought to be devoted to the common welfare, but the state is permitted to pursue its own interest without regard to the welfare of other nations. But quite aside from the fact that the doctrines of totalitarianism are disguises for the most extreme selfishness, they are a revival—in secular language—of the religious idea of intrinsic human powerlessness and impotence and the resulting need for submission, to overcome which was the essence of modern spiritual and political progress. Not only do the authoritarian ideologies threaten the most precious achievement of Western culture, the respect for the uniqueness and dignity of the individual; they also tend to block the way to constructive criticism of modern society, and thereby to necessary changes. The failure of modern culture lies not in its principle of individualism, not in the idea that moral virtue is the same as the pursuit of self-interest, but in the deterioration of the meaning of self-interest; not in the fact that people are *too much concerned with their self-interest*, but that they are *not concerned enough with the interest of their real self; not in the fact that they are too selfish, but that they do not love themselves.*

If the causes for persevering in the pursuit of a fictitious idea of self-interest are as deeply rooted in the contemporary social structure as indicated above, the chances for a change in the meaning of self-interest would seem to be remote indeed, unless one can point to specific factors operating in the direction of change.

Perhaps the most important factor is the inner dissatisfaction of modern man with the results of his pursuit of "self-interest." The religion of success is crumbling and becoming a façade itself. The social "open spaces" grow narrower; the failure of the hopes for a better world after the First World War, the depression at the end of the twenties, the threat of a new and immensely destructive war so shortly after the Second World War, and the boundless insecurity resulting from this threat, shake the faith in the pursuit of this form of self-interest. Aside from these factors, the worship of success itself has failed to satisfy man's ineradicable striving to be himself. Like so many fantasies and daydreams, this one too fulfilled its function only for a time, as long as it was new, as long as the excitement connected with it was strong enough to keep man from considering it soberly. There is an increasing number of people to whom everything they are doing seems futile. They are still under the spell of the slogans which preach faith in the secular paradise of success and glamour. But doubt, the fertile condition of all progress, has begun to beset them and has made them ready to ask what their real self-interest as human beings is.

This inner disillusionment and the readiness for a revaluation of self-interest could hardly become effective unless the economic conditions of our culture permitted it. I have pointed out that while the canalizing of all human energy into work and the striving for success was one of the indispensable conditions of the enormous achievement of modern capitalism, a stage has been reached where the problem of *production* has been virtually solved and where the problem of the *organization* of social life has become the paramount task of mankind. Man has created such sources of mechanical energy that he has freed himself from the task of putting all his human energy into work in order to produce the material conditions for living. He could spend a considerable part of his energy on the task of living itself.

Only if these two conditions, the subjective dissatisfaction with a culturally patterned aim and the socioeconomic basis for a change, are present, can an indispensable third factor, rational insight, become effective. This holds true as a principle of social and psychological change in general and of the change in the meaning of self-interest in particular. The time has come when the anesthetized striving for the pursuit of man's real interest is coming to life again. Once man knows what his self-interest is, the first, and the most difficult, step to its realization has been taken.

2. Conscience, Man's Recall to Himself

Whoever talks about and reflects upon an evil thing he has done, is thinking the vileness he has perpetrated, and what one thinks, therein is one caught—with one's whole soul one is caught utterly in what one thinks, and so he is still caught in vileness. And he will surely not be able to turn, for his spirit will coarsen and his heart rot, and besides this, a sad mood may come upon him. What would you? Stir filth this way or that, and it is still filth. To have sinned or not to have sinned— what does it profit us in heaven? In the time I am brooding on this, I could be stringing pearls for the joy of heaven. That is why it is written: "Depart from evil, and do good"— turn wholly from evil, do not brood in its way,

and do good. You have done wrong? Then
balance it by doing right.

                              Isaac Meier of Ger[31]

There is no prouder statement man can make
than to say: "I shall act according to my conscience." Throughout history men have upheld the
principles of justice, love, and truth against every
kind of pressure brought to bear upon them in
order to make them relinquish what they knew
and believed. The prophets acted according to
their conscience when they denounced their country and predicted its downfall because of its cor-
ruption and injustice. Socrates preferred death
to a course in which he would have betrayed his
conscience by compromising with the truth. Without the existence of conscience, the human race
would have bogged down long ago in its hazardous
course.

Different from these men are others who also
have claimed to be motivated by their conscience:
the men of the Inquisition who burned men of
conscience at the stake, claiming to do so in the
name of *their* conscience; the predatory war-
makers claiming to act on behalf of their conscience when they put their lust for power above
all other considerations. In fact, there is hardly
any act of cruelty or indifference against others
or oneself which has not been rationalized as the
dictate of conscience, thus showing the power
of conscience in its need to be placated.

Conscience in its various empirical manifestations is indeed confusing. Are these various kinds
of conscience the same, with only their *contents*
differing? Are they different phenomena with only
the name "conscience" in common? Or does the
assumption of the existence of conscience turn

[31] *In Time and Eternity*, ed. by N. N. Glatzer (New York:
Schocken Books, 1946).

out to be untenable when we investigate the phenomenon empirically as a problem of human motivation?

To these questions, the philosophical literature
on conscience brings a wealth of clues. Cicero and
Seneca speak of conscience as the inner voice
which accuses and defends our conduct with respect to its ethical qualities. Stoic philosophy relates it to self-preservation (taking care of
oneself), and it is described by Chrysippus as the
consciousness of harmony within oneself. In
scholastic philosophy, conscience is considered to
be the law of reason (*lex rationis*) implanted in
man by God. It is differentiated from "synderesis"; while the latter is the habit (or faculty)
of judging, and of willing the right, the former
applies the general principle to particular actions.
Although the term "synderesis" has been dropped
by modern writers, the term "conscience" is used
frequently for what scholastic philosophy had
meant by synderesis, the inner awareness of moral
principles. The emotional element in this awareness was stressed by English writers. Shaftes-
bury, for instance, assumed the existence of a
"moral sense" in man, a sense of right and wrong,
an emotional reaction, based on the fact that the
mind of man is itself in harmony with the cosmic
order. Butler proposed that moral principles are
an intrinsic part of the constitution of man and
identified conscience particularly with the innate
desire for benevolent action. Our feelings for
others and our reaction to their approval or disapproval are the core of conscience according to
Adam Smith. Kant abstracted conscience from all
specific contents and identified it with the sense
of duty as such. Nietzsche, a bitter critic of the
religious "bad conscience," saw genuine conscience
rooted in self-affirmation, in the ability to "say
yes to one's self." Max Scheler believed conscience

to be the expression of rational judgment, but a judgment by feeling and not by thought.

But important problems are still left unanswered and untouched, problems of motivation on which the data of psychoanalytic research may shed some more light. In the following discussion we shall distinguish between "authoritarian" and "humanistic" conscience, a differentiation which follows the general line of distinction between authoritarian and humanistic ethics.

A. AUTHORITARIAN CONSCIENCE

The authoritarian conscience is the voice of an internalized external authority, the parents, the state, or whoever the authorities in a culture happen to be. As long as people's relationships to the authorities remain external, without ethical sanction, we can hardly speak of conscience; such conduct is merely expediential, regulated by fear of punishment and hope for reward, always dependent on the presence of these authorities, on their knowledge of what one is doing, and their alleged or real ability to punish and to reward. Often an experience which people take to be a feeling of guilt springing from their conscience is really nothing but their fear of such authorities. Properly speaking, these people do not feel *guilty* but *afraid*. In the formation of conscience, however, such authorities as the parents, the church, the state, public opinion are either consciously or unconsciously accepted as ethical and moral legislators whose laws and sanctions one adopts, thus internalizing them. The laws and sanctions of external authority become part of oneself, as it were, and instead of feeling responsible to something outside oneself, one feels responsible to something inside, to one's *conscience*. Conscience is a more effective regulator of conduct than fear of external authorities; for, while one can run away from the latter, one can not escape from oneself nor, therefore, from the internalized authority which has become part of oneself. The authoritarian conscience is what Freud has described as the Super-Ego; but as I shall show later, this is only one form of conscience or, possibly, a preliminary stage in the development of conscience.

While authoritarian conscience is different from fear of punishment and hope for reward, the relationship to the authority having become internalized, it is not very different in other essential respects. The most important point of similarity is the fact that the prescriptions of authoritarian conscience are not determined by one's own *value judgment* but exclusively by the fact that its commands and tabus are pronounced by authorities. If these norms happen to be good, conscience will guide man's action in the direction of the good. However, they have not become the norms of conscience *because* they are good, but because they are the norms given by authority. If they are bad, they are just as much part of conscience. A believer in Hitler, for instance, felt he was acting according to *his* conscience when he committed acts that were humanly revolting.

But even though the relationship to authority becomes internalized, this internalization must not be imagined to be so complete as to divorce conscience from the external authorities. Such complete divorcement, which we can study in cases of obsessional neurosis, is the exception rather than the rule; normally, the person whose conscience is authoritarian is bound to the external authorities *and* to their internalized echo. In fact, there is a constant interaction between the two. The presence of external authorities by whom a person is awed is the source which continuously nourishes the internalized authority, the conscience. If the authorities did not exist in reality, that is, if the person had no reason to be afraid of them, then the authoritarian conscience would weaken and lose power. Simultaneously, the conscience influences the image which a person has of the external authorities. For such conscience is always colored by man's need to admire, to have some ideal,[32] to strive for some kind of perfection, and the image of perfection is projected upon the external authorities. The result is that the picture of these authorities is, in turn, colored by the "ideal" aspect of conscience. This is very important because the concept a person has of the qualities of the authorities differs from their real qualities; it becomes more and more idealized and, therefore, more apt to be re-internalized.[33] Very often this interaction of internalization and projection results in an unshakable conviction in the ideal character of the authority, a conviction which is immune to all contradictory empirical evidence.

The contents of the authoritarian conscience are derived from the commands and tabus of the authority; its strength is rooted in the emotions of fear of, and admiration for, the authority. *Good conscience is consciousness of pleasing the (external and internalized) authority; guilty conscience is the consciousness of displeasing it.* The good (authoritarian) conscience produces a feeling of well-being and security, for it implies approval by, and greater closeness to, the authority; the guilty conscience produces fear and insecurity, because acting against the will of the authority implies the danger of being punished and—what is worse—of being deserted by the authority.

[32] This side was stressed by Freud in his early concept of the "Ego Ideal."

[33] A more detailed analysis of the relationship of conscience and authority is to be found in my discussion of the subject in *Studien ueber Autoritaet und Familie*, ed. by M. Horkheimer (Paris: Félix Alcan, 1936).

In order to understand the full impact of the last statement we must remember the character structure of the authoritarian person. He has found inner security by becoming, symbiotically, part of an authority felt to be greater and more powerful than himself. As long as he is part of that authority—at the expense of his own integrity—he feels that he is participating in the authority's strength. His feeling of certainty and identity depends on this symbiosis; to be rejected by the authority means to be thrown into a void, to face the horror of nothingness. Anything, to the authoritarian character, is better than this. To be sure, the love and approval of the authority give him the greatest satisfaction; but even punishment is better than rejection. The punishing authority is still with him, and if he has "sinned," the punishment is at least proof that the authority still cares. By his acceptance of the punishment his sin is wiped out and the security of belonging is restored.

The Biblical report of Cain's crime and punishment offers a classic illustration of the fact that what man is most afraid of is not punishment but rejection. God accepted Abel's offerings but did not accept Cain's. Without giving any reason, God did to Cain the worst thing that can be done to a man who can not live without being acceptable to an authority. He refused his offering and thus rejected *him*. The rejection was unbearable for Cain, so Cain killed the rival who had deprived him of the indispensable. What was Cain's punishment? He was not killed or even harmed; as a matter of fact, God forbade anyone to kill him (the mark of Cain was meant to protect him from being killed). His punishment was to be made an *outcast;* after God had rejected him, he was then separated from his fellow men. This punishment was indeed one of which Cain had to say: "My punishment is greater than I can bear."

So far I have dealt with the formal structure of the authoritarian conscience by showing that the good conscience is the consciousness of pleasing the (external and internalized) authorities; the guilty conscience, the consciousness of displeasing them. We turn now to the question of what the *contents* of good and of guilty authoritarian conscience are. While it is obvious that any transgression of positive norms postulated by the authority constitutes disobedience and, therefore, guilt (regardless of whether or not these norms in themselves are good or bad), there are offenses which are intrinsic to any authoritarian situation.

The prime offense in the authoritarian situation is rebellion against the authority's rule. Thus disobedience becomes the "cardinal sin"; obedience, the cardinal virtue. Obedience implies the recognition of the authority's superior power and wisdom; his right to command, to reward, and to punish according to his own fiats. The authority demands submission not only because of the fear of its power but out of the conviction of its moral superiority and right. The respect due the authority carries with it the tabu on questioning it. The authority may deign to give explanations for his commands and prohibitions, his rewards and punishments, or he may refrain from doing so; but never has the individual the *right* to question or to criticize. If there seem to be any reasons for criticizing the authority, it is the individual subject to the authority who must be at fault; and the mere fact that such an individual dares to criticize is *ipso facto* proof that he is guilty.

The duty of recognizing the authority's superiority results in several prohibitions. The most comprehensive of these is the tabu against feeling oneself to be, or ever able to become, *like* the authority, for this would contradict the latter's unqualified superiority and uniqueness. The real sin of Adam and Eve is, as has been pointed out before, the attempt to become like God; and it is as punishment for this challenge and simultaneously as deterrence of a repetition of it that they are expelled from the Garden of Eden.[34] In authoritarian systems the authority is made out to be fundamentally different from his subjects. He has powers not attainable by anyone else: magic, wisdom, strength which can never be matched by his subjects. Whatever the authority's prerogatives are, whether he is the master of the universe or a unique leader sent by fate, the fundamental inequality between him and man is the basic tenet of authoritarian conscience. One particularly important aspect of the uniqueness of the authority is the privilege of being the only one who does not follow another's will, but who himself wills; who is not a means but an end in himself; who creates and is not created. In the authoritarian orientation, the power of will and creation are the privilege of the authority. Those subject to him are means to his end and, consequently, his property and used by him for his own purposes. The supremacy of the authority is questioned by the attempt of the creature to cease being a *thing* and to become a creator.

But man has never yet ceased striving to produce and to create because productiveness is the source of strength, freedom, and happiness. However, to the extent to which he feels dependent on powers transcending him, his very productiveness, the assertion of his will, makes him feel guilty. The men of Babel were punished for trying by the efforts of a unified human race to build a city reaching to heaven. Prometheus was chained to the rock for having given man the secret of fire,

[34] The idea that man is created in "God's image" transcends the authoritarian structure of this part of the Old Testament and is in fact the other pole around which Judaeo-Christian religion has developed, particularly in its mystical representatives.

symbolizing productiveness. Pride in the power and strength of man was denounced by Luther and Calvin as sinful pride; by political dictators, as criminal individualism. Man tried to appease the gods for the crime of productiveness by sacrifices, by giving them the best of the crop or of the herd. Circumcision is another attempt at such appeasement; part of the phallus, the symbol of male creativeness, is sacrificed to God so that man may retain the right to its use. In addition to sacrifices in which man pays tribute to the gods by acknowledging—if only symbolically—their monopoly on productiveness, man curbs his own powers by feelings of guilt, rooted in the authoritarian conviction that the exercise of his own will and creative power is a rebellion against the authority's prerogatives to be the sole creator and that the subjects' duty is to be his "things." This feeling of guilt, in turn, weakens man, reduces his power, and increases his submission in order to atone for his attempt to be his "own creator and builder."

Paradoxically, the authoritarian *guilty* conscience is a result of the feeling of strength, independence, productiveness, and pride, while the authoritarian *good* conscience springs from the feeling of obedience, dependence, powerlessness, and sinfulness. St. Paul, Augustine, Luther, and Calvin have described this good conscience in unmistakable terms. To be aware of one's powerlessness, to despise oneself, to be burdened by the feeling of one's own sinfulness and wickedness are the signs of goodness. The very fact of having a guilty conscience is in itself a sign of one's virtue because the guilty conscience is the symptom of one's "fear and trembling" before the authority. The paradoxical result is that the (authoritarian) *guilty conscience becomes the basis for a "good" conscience, while the good conscience, if one should have it, ought to create a feeling of guilt.*

The internalization of authority has two implications: one, which we have just discussed, where man submits to the authority; the other, where he takes over the role of the authority by treating himself with the same strictness and cruelty. Man thus becomes not only the obedient slave but also the strict taskmaster who treats himself as his own slave. This second implication is very important for the understanding of the psychological mechanism of authoritarian conscience. The authoritarian character, being more or less crippled in his productiveness, develops a certain amount of sadism and destructiveness.[35] These destructive energies are discharged by taking over the role of the authority and dominating oneself as the servant. In the analysis of the Super-Ego, Freud has given a description of its destructive components which has been amply confirmed by clinical data collected by other observers. It does not matter whether one assumes, as Freud did in his earlier writings, that the root of aggression is to be found mainly in instinctual frustration or, as he assumed later, in the "death-instinct." What matters is the fact that the authoritarian conscience is fed by destructiveness against the person's own self so that destructive strivings are thus permitted to operate under the disguise of virtue. Psychoanalytic exploration, especially of the obsessional character, reveals the degree of cruelty and destructiveness conscience sometimes has, and how it enables one to act out the lingering hate by turning it against oneself. Freud has convincingly demonstrated the correctness of Nietzsche's thesis that the blockage of freedom turns man's instincts "backward against man himself. Enmity, cruelty, the delight in persecution, in surprises, change, destruction—the turning of

[35] F. Nietzsche, *The Genealogy of Morals*, II, 16.

all these instincts against their own possessors: this is the origin of the 'bad conscience.' "[36]

Most religious and political systems in the history of mankind could serve as illustrations of the authoritarian conscience. Since I have analyzed Protestantism and Fascism from this point of view in *Escape from Freedom* I shall not give historical illustrations here, but shall limit myself to the discussion of some aspects of the authoritarian conscience as they can be observed in the parent-child relationships in our culture.

The use of the term "authoritarian conscience" in reference to our culture may surprise the reader, since we are accustomed to think of authoritarian attitudes as being characteristic only of authoritarian, nondemocratic cultures; but such a view underestimates the strength of authoritarian elements, especially the role of anonymous authority operating in the contemporary family and society.[37]

The psychoanalytic interview is one of the vantage points for studying the authoritarian conscience in the urban middle class. Here parental authority and the way children cope with it are revealed as being the crucial problem of neurosis. The analyst finds many patients incapable of criticizing their parents at all; others, who, while criticizing their parents in some respects, stop short of criticizing them with regard to those qualities they themselves have suffered from; still others feel guilty and anxious when they express pertinent criticism or rage against one of their parents. It often takes considerable analytic work to enable a person even to remember incidents which provoked his anger and criticism.[38]

---

[36] *Ibid.*, II, 16.

[37] Cf. the discussion of anonymous authority in democratic society in *Escape from Freedom*, Chap. V, p. 3.

[38] F. Kafka's letter to his father, in which he tried to explain to him why he had always been afraid of him is

More subtle and still more hidden are those guilt feelings which result from the experience of not pleasing one's parents. Sometimes the child's feeling of guilt is attached to the fact of his not loving the parents sufficiently, particularly when the parents expect to be the focus of the child's feelings. Sometimes it arises from the fear of having disappointed parental expectations. The latter point is particularly important because it refers to one of the crucial elements in the attitude of the parent in the authoritarian family. In spite of the great difference between the Roman pater-familias, whose family was his property, and the modern father, the feeling that children are brought into the world to satisfy the parents and compensate them for the disappointments of their own lives is still widespread. This attitude has found its classic expression in *Creon's* famous speech on parental authority in Sophocles' "Antigone":

> "So it is right, my son, to be disposed—
> In everything to back your father's quarrel.
> It is for this men pray to breed and rear
> In their homes *dutiful offspring*—to requite
> The foe with evil, and their father's friend
> Honour, as did their father. Whoso gets
> Children *unserviceable*—what else could he
> Be said to breed, but troubles for himself,
> And store of laughter for his enemies."[39]

Even in our nonauthoritarian culture, it happens that parents want their children to be "service-able" in order to make up for what the parents missed in life. If the parents are not successful, the children should attain success so as to give

a classic document in this respect. Cf. A. Franz Kafka, *Miscellany* (New York: Twice a Year Press, 1940).

[39] *The Complete Greek Drama*, ed. by W. J. Oates and E. O'Neill, Jr., Vol. I (New York: Random House, 1938).

them a vicarious satisfaction. If they do not feel loved (particularly if the parents do not love each other), the children are to make up for it; if they feel powerless in their social life, they want to have the satisfaction of controlling and dominating their children. Even if the children fall in with these expectations, they still feel guilty for not doing enough and thus disappointing their parents.

One particularly subtle form which the feeling of disappointing the parents frequently takes is caused by the feeling of being different. Dominating parents want their children to be like them in temperament and character. The choleric father, for instance, is out of sympathy with a phlegmatic son; the father interested in practical achievements is disappointed by a son interested in ideas and theoretical inquiry, and vice versa. If the father's attitude is proprietary, he interprets the son's *difference* from him as inferiority; the son feels guilty and inferior because of his being different and he tries to make himself into the kind of person his father wants him to be; but he succeeds only in crippling his own growth and in becoming a very imperfect replica of his father. Since he believes he ought to be like his father, this failure gives him a guilty conscience. The son, in attempting to free himself from these notions of obligation and to become "himself," is frequently so heavily weighed down by a burden of guilt over this "crime" that he falls by the wayside before ever reaching his goal of freedom. The burden is so heavy because he has to cope not only with his parents, with their disappointment, accusations, and appeals, but also with the whole culture which expects children to "love" their parents. The foregoing description, though fitting the authoritarian family, does not seem to be correct as far as the contemporary American, especially the urban, family is concerned in which we find little overt authority. But the picture I have given holds true, nevertheless, in its essential points. Instead of overt we find anonymous authority expressed in terms of emotionally highly charged expectations instead of explicit commands. Moreover, the parents do not feel themselves to be authorities, but nevertheless they are the representatives of the anonymous authority of the market, and they expect the children to live up to standards to which both—the parents and the children—submit.

Not only do guilt feelings result from one's dependence on an irrational authority and from the feeling that it is one's duty to please that authority but the guilt feeling in its turn reinforces dependence. Guilt feelings have proved to be the most effective means of forming and increasing dependency, and herein lies one of the social functions of authoritarian ethics throughout history. The authority as lawgiver makes its subjects feel guilty for their many and unavoidable transgressions. The guilt of unavoidable transgressions before authority and the need for its forgiveness thus creates an endless chain of offense, guilt feeling, and the need for absolution which keeps the subject in bondage and grateful for forgiveness rather than critical of the authority's demands. It is this interaction between guilt feeling and dependency which makes for the solidity and strength of the authoritarian relationships. The dependence on irrational authority results in a weakening of will in the dependent person and, at the same time, whatever tends to paralyze the will makes for an increase in dependence. Thus a vicious circle is formed.

The most effective method for weakening the child's will is to arouse his sense of guilt. This is done early by making the child feel that his sexual strivings and their early manifestations are "bad." Since the child can not help having sexual strivings, this method of arousing guilt can hardly fail. Once parents (and society represented by them) have succeeded in making the association of sex and guilt permanent, guilt feelings are produced to the same degree, and with the same constancy as sexual impulses occur. In addition, other physical functions are blighted by "moral" considerations. If the child does not go to the toilet in the prescribed fashion, if he is not as clean as expected, if he does not eat what he is supposed to— he is *bad*. At the age of five or six the child has acquired an all-pervasive sense of guilt because the conflict between his natural impulses and their moral evaluation by his parents constitutes a constantly generating source of guilt feelings.

Liberal and "progressive" systems of education have not changed this situation as much as one would like to think. Overt authority has been replaced by anonymous authority, overt commands by "scientifically" established formulas; "don't do this" by "you will not like to do this." In fact, in many ways this anonymous authority may be even more oppressive than the overt one. The child is no longer aware of being bossed (nor are the parents of giving orders), and he cannot fight back and thus develop a sense of independence. He is coaxed and persuaded in the name of science, common sense, and cooperation—and who can fight against such objective principles?

Once the will of the child has been broken, his sense of guilt is reinforced in still another way. He is dimly aware of his submission and defeat, and he must make sense of it. He cannot accept a puzzling and painful experience without trying to explain it. The rationalization in this case is, in principle, the same as that of the Indian untouchable or the suffering Christian—his defeat and weakness are "explained" as being just punishment for his sins. The fact of his loss of freedom is rationalized as proof of guilt, and this conviction increases the guilt feeling induced by the cultural and parental systems of value.

The child's natural reaction to the pressure of parental authority is rebellion, which is the essence of Freud's "Oedipus complex." Freud thought that, say, the little boy, because of his sexual desire for his mother, becomes the rival of his father, and that the neurotic development consists in the failure to cope in a satisfactory way with the anxiety rooted in this rivalry. In pointing to the conflict between the child and parental authority and the child's failure to solve this conflict satisfactorily, Freud did touch upon the roots of neurosis; in my opinion, however, this conflict is not brought about primarily by the sexual rivalry but results from the child's reaction to the pressure of parental authority, which in itself is an intrinsic part of patriarchal society.

Inasmuch as social and parental authority tend to break his will, spontaneity, and independence, the child, not being born to be broken, fights against the authority represented by his parents; he fights for his freedom not only *from* pressure, but also for his freedom to be himself, a full-fledged human being, not an automaton. For some children the battle for freedom will be more successful than for others, although only a few succeed entirely. The scars left from the child's defeat in the fight against irrational authority are to be found at the bottom of every neurosis. They form a syndrome the most important features of which are the weakening or paralysis of the person's originality and spontaneity; the weakening of the self and the substitution of a pseudo self in which the feeling of "I am" is dulled and replaced by the experience of self as the sum total of others' expectations; the substitution of autonomy by heteronomy; the fogginess or, to use H. S. Sullivan's term, the parataxic quality of all interpersonal experiences. The most important symptom of the defeat in the fight for oneself is the guilty conscience. If one has not succeeded in breaking out of the authoritarian net, the unsuccessful attempt to escape is proof of guilt, and only by renewed submission can the good conscience be regained.

B. HUMANISTIC CONSCIENCE

Humanistic conscience is not the internalized voice of an authority whom we are eager to please and afraid of displeasing; it is our own voice, present in every human being and independent of external sanctions and rewards. What is the nature of this voice? Why do we hear it and why can we become deaf to it?

Humanistic conscience is the reaction of our total personality to its proper functioning or dysfunctioning; not a reaction to the functioning of this or that capacity but to the totality of capacities which constitute our human and our individual existence. Conscience judges our functioning as human beings; it is (as the root of the word *con-scientia* indicates) *knowledge within oneself,* knowledge of our respective success or failure in the art of living. But although conscience is *knowledge,* it is more than mere knowledge in the realm of abstract thought. It has an *affective* quality, for it is the reaction of our total personality and not only the reaction of our mind. In fact, we need not be aware of what our conscience says in order to be influenced by it.

Actions, thoughts, and feelings which are conducive to the proper functioning and unfolding of our total personality produce a feeling of inner approval, of "rightness," characteristic of the humanistic "good conscience." On the other hand, acts, thoughts, and feelings injurious to our total personality produce a feeling of uneasiness and discomfort, characteristic of the "guilty conscience." *Conscience is thus a re-action of our-selves to ourselves*. It is the voice of our true selves which summons us back to ourselves, to live pro-ductively, to develop fully and harmoniously—that is, *to become what we potentially are*. It is the guardian of our integrity; it is the "ability to guarantee one's self with all due pride, and also at the same time *to say yes* to one's self."[40] If love can be defined as the affirmation of the potentialities and the care for, and the respect of, the uniqueness of the loved person, humanistic conscience can be justly called *the voice of our loving care for ourselves*.

Humanistic conscience represents not only the expression of our true selves; it contains also the essence of our moral experiences in life. In it we preserve the knowledge of our aim in life and of the principles through which to attain it; those principles which we have discovered ourselves as well as those we have learned from others and which we have found to be true.

Humanistic conscience is the expression of man's self-interest and integrity, while author-itarian conscience is concerned with man's obedi-ence, self-sacrifice, duty, or his "social adjust-ment." The goal of humanistic conscience is productiveness and, therefore, happiness, since happiness is the necessary concomitant of produc-tive living. To cripple oneself by becoming a tool of others, no matter how dignified they are made to appear, to be "selfless," unhappy, resigned, discouraged, is in opposition to the demands of one's conscience; any violation of the integrity and proper functioning of our personality, with regard to thinking as well as acting, and even with regard to such matters as taste for food or sexual behavior is acting against one's conscience.

---

[40] F. Nietzsche, *The Genealogy of Morals*, II, 3. Cf. also Heidegger's description of conscience in M. Heidegger, *Sein und Zeit*, 54–60, Halle a.s., 1927.

But is our analysis of conscience not contradicted by the fact that in many people its voice is so feeble as not to be heard and acted upon? Indeed, this fact is the reason for the moral precariousness of the human situation. If conscience always spoke loudly and distinctly enough, only a few would be misled from their moral objective. One answer follows from the very nature of conscience itself: since its function is to be the guardian of man's true self-interest, it is alive to the extent to which a person has not lost himself entirely and become the prey of his own indifference and destructiveness. Its relation to one's own productiveness is one of interaction. The more productively one lives, the stronger is one's conscience, and, in turn, the more it furthers one's productiveness. The less productively one lives, the weaker becomes one's conscience; the paradoxical—and tragic—situation of man is that his conscience is weakest when he needs it most.

Another answer to the question of the relative ineffectiveness of conscience is our refusal to listen and—what is even more important—our ignorance of knowing how to listen. People often are under the illusion that their conscience will speak with a loud voice and its message will be clear and distinct; waiting for such a voice, they do not hear anything. But when the voice of conscience is feeble, it is indistinct; and one has to learn how to listen and to understand its communications in order to act accordingly.

However, learning to understand the communications of one's conscience is exceedingly difficult, mainly for two reasons. In order to listen to the voice of our conscience, we must be able to listen to ourselves, and this is exactly what most people in our culture have difficulties in doing. We listen to every voice and to everybody but not to ourselves. We are constantly exposed to the noise of opinions and ideas hammering at us from everywhere: motion pictures, newspapers, radio, idle chatter. If we had planned intentionally to prevent ourselves from ever listening to ourselves, we could have done no better.

Listening to oneself is so difficult because this art requires another ability, rare in modern man: that of being alone with oneself. In fact, we have developed a phobia of being alone; we prefer the most trivial and even obnoxious company, the most meaningless activities, to being alone with ourselves; we seem to be frightened at the prospect of facing ourselves. Is it because we feel we would be such bad company? I think the fear of being alone with ourselves is rather a feeling of embarrassment, bordering sometimes on terror at seeing a person at once so well known and so strange; we are afraid and run away. We thus miss the chance of listening to ourselves, and we continue to ignore our conscience.

Listening to the feeble and indistinct voice of our conscience is difficult also because it does not speak to us directly but indirectly and because we are often not aware that it is our conscience which disturbs us. We may feel only anxious (or even sick) for a number of reasons which have no apparent connection with our conscience. Perhaps the most frequent indirect reaction of our conscience to being neglected is a vague and unspecific feeling of guilt and uneasiness, or simply a feeling of tiredness or listlessness. Sometimes such feelings are rationalized as guilt feelings for not having done this or that, when actually the omissions one feels guilty about do not constitute genuine moral problems. But if the genuine though unconscious feeling of guilt has become too strong to be silenced by superficial rationalizations, it finds expression in deeper and more intense anxieties and even in physical or mental sickness.

One form of this anxiety is the fear of death;

not the normal fear of having to die which every human being experiences in the contemplation of death, but a horror of dying by which people can be possessed constantly. This irrational fear of death results from the failure of having lived; it is the expression of our guilty conscience for having wasted our life and missed the chance of productive use of our capacities. To die is poignantly bitter, but the idea of having to die without having lived is unbearable. Related to the irrational fear of death is the fear of growing old by which even more people in our culture are haunted. Here, too, we find a reasonable and normal apprehension of old age which, however, is very different in quality and intensity from the nightmarish dread of "being too old." Frequently we can observe people, especially in the analytic situation, who are obsessed by the fear of old age when they are quite young; they are convinced that the waning of physical strength is linked with the weakening of their total personality, their emotional and intellectual powers. This idea is hardly more than a superstition, which persists in spite of the overwhelming evidence to the contrary. It is fostered, in our culture, by the emphasis on so-called youthful qualities, like quickness, adaptability, and physical vigor, which are the qualities needed in a world primarily orientated to success in competition rather than to the development of one's character. But many examples show that the person who lives productively before he is old by no means deteriorates; on the contrary, the mental and emotional qualities he developed in the process of productive living continue to grow although physical vigor wanes. The unproductive person, however, indeed deteriorates in his whole personality when his physical vigor, which had been the main spring of his activities, dries up. The decay of the personality in old age is a symptom: it is the proof of the failure of hav-

ing lived productively. The fear of getting old
is an expression of the feeling—often unconscious
—of living unproductively; it is a reaction of our
conscience to the mutilation of our selves. There
are cultures in which there is a greater need and,
therefore, a higher esteem for, the specific qualities of old age, like wisdom and experience. In
such cultures can we find an attitude which is so
beautifully expressed in the following utterance
of the Japanese painter Hokusai:

> From the age of six I had a mania for
> drawing the form of things. By the time I
> was fifty I had published an infinity of de-
> signs; but all I have produced before the age
> of seventy is not worth taking into account.
> At seventy-three I have learned a little about
> the real structure of nature, of animals,
> plants, birds, fishes and insects. In con-
> sequence when I am eighty, I shall have made
> more progress; at ninety I shall penetrate
> the mystery of things; at a hundred I shall
> certainly have reached a marvelous stage;
> and when I am a hundred and ten, everything
> I do, be it but a dot or a line, will be alive.
> Written at the age of seventy-five by me,
> once Hokusai, today Gwakio Rojin, the old
> man mad about drawing.[41]

The fear of disapproval, though less dramatic
than the irrational fear of death and of old age,
is a hardly less significant expression of unconscious guilt feeling. Here also we find the irrational distortion of a normal attitude: man
naturally wants to be accepted by his fellows;
but modern man wants to be accepted by everybody and therefore is afraid to deviate, in think-

[41] From J. LaFarge, *A Talk About Hokusai* (W. C.
Martin, 1896).

ing, feeling, and acting, from the cultural pattern. One reason among others for this irrational fear of disapproval is an unconscious guilt feeling. If man cannot approve of himself because he fails in the task of living productively, he has to substitute approval by others for approval by himself. This craving for approval can be fully understood only if we recognize it as a moral problem, as the expression of the all-pervasive though unconscious guilt feeling.

It would seem that man can successfully shut himself off against hearing the voice of his conscience. But there is one state of existence in which this attempt fails, and that is sleep. Here he is shut off from the noise hammering at him in the daytime and receptive only to his inner experience, which is made up of many irrational strivings as well as value judgments and insights. Sleep is often the only occasion in which man cannot silence his conscience; but the tragedy of it is that when we do hear our conscience speak in sleep we cannot act, and that, when able to act, we forget what we knew in our dream.

The following dream may serve as an illustration. A well-known writer was offered a position where he would have had to sell his integrity as a writer in exchange for a great deal of money and fame; while considering whether or not to accept the offer, he had this dream: At the foot of a mountain, he sees two very successful men whom he despises for their opportunism; they tell him to drive up the narrow road to the peak. He follows their advice and, when almost on the top of the mountain, his car falls off the road, and he is killed. The message of his dream needs little interpretation: while he slept, he knew that the acceptance of the offered position would be equivalent to destruction; not, of course, to his physical death, as the symbolic language of the dream expresses it, but to his destruction as an integrated, productive human being.

In our discussion of conscience I have examined the authoritarian and humanistic conscience separately in order to show their characteristic qualities; but they are, of course, not separated in reality and not mutually exclusive in any one person. On the contrary, actually everybody has both "consciences." The problem is to distinguish their respective strength and their interrelation.

Often guilt feelings are consciously experienced in terms of the authoritarian conscience while, dynamically, they are rooted in the humanistic conscience; in this case the authoritarian conscience is a rationalization, as it were, of the humanistic conscience. A person may feel consciously guilty for not pleasing authorities, while unconsciously he feels guilty for not living up to his own expectations of himself. A man, for instance, who had wanted to become a musician had instead become a businessman to satisfy his father's wishes. He is rather unsuccessful in business, and his father gives vent to his disappointment at the son's failure. The son, feeling depressed and incapable of doing adequate work, eventually decides to seek the help of a psychoanalyst. In the analytic interview he speaks first at great length about his feelings of inadequacy and depression. Soon he recognizes that his depression is caused by his guilt feelings for having disappointed his father. When the analyst questions the genuineness of this guilt feeling, the patient is annoyed. But soon afterward he sees himself in a dream as a very successful businessman, praised by his father, something which had never occurred in real life; at this point in the dream he, the dreamer, is suddenly seized by panic and by the impulse to kill himself, and he wakes up. He is startled by his dream and considers whether he is not mistaken after all about the real source of his guilt feeling. He then discovers that the core of his guilt feeling is not the failure to satisfy his father, but, on the contrary, his obedience to him and his failure to satisfy himself. His conscious guilt feeling is genuine enough, as far as it goes, as an expression of his authoritarian conscience; but it covers up the bulk of his feeling of guilt toward himself of which he was completely unaware. The reasons for this repression are not difficult to discern: the patterns of our culture support this repression; according to them it makes sense to feel guilty for disappointing one's father, but it makes little sense to feel guilty for neglecting one's self. Another reason is the fear that by becoming aware of his real guilt, he would be forced to emancipate himself and to take *his* life seriously instead of oscillating between the fear of his angry father and the attempts to satisfy him.

Another form of the relation between an authoritarian and humanistic conscience is that in which, although the contents of norms are identical, the motivation for their acceptance differs. The commands, for instance, not to kill, not to hate, not to be envious, and to love one's neighbor are norms of authoritarian as well as of humanistic ethics. It may be said that in the first stage of the evolution of conscience the authority gives commands which later on are followed not because of submission to the authority but because of one's responsibility to oneself. Julian Huxley has pointed out that acquisition of an authoritarian conscience was a stage in the process of human evolution necessary before rationality and freedom had developed to an extent which made humanistic conscience possible; others have stated this same idea with regard to the development of the child. While Huxley is right in his historical analysis, I do not believe that with regard to the child, in a nonauthoritarian society, the authoritarian conscience has to exist as a precondition for the formation of humanistic conscience; but only the future development of mankind can prove or disprove the validity of this assumption.

If the conscience is based upon rigid and unassailable irrational authority, the development of humanistic conscience can be almost entirely suppressed. Man, then, becomes completely dependent on powers outside himself and ceases to care or to feel responsible for his own existence. All that matters to him is the approval or disapproval by these powers, which can be the state, a leader, or a no less powerful public opinion. Even the most unethical behavior—in the humanistic sense—can be experienced as "duty" in the authoritarian sense. The feeling of "oughtness," common to both, is so deceptive a factor because it can refer to the worst as well as to the best in man.

A beautiful illustration of the complex interrelation of authoritarian and humanistic conscience is Kafka's *The Trial.* The hero of the book, K, finds himself "arrested one fine morning" for a crime of which he is ignorant and is kept so for the remaining year he is to live. The entire novel deals with K's attempt to plead his case before a mysterious court whose laws and procedure he does not know. He tries frantically to engage the help of shyster lawyers, of women connected with the court, of anyone he can find—all to no avail. Eventually he is sentenced to death and executed.

The novel is written in dreamlike, symbolic language; all the events are concrete and seemingly realistic, although they actually refer to inner experiences symbolized by external events. The story expresses the sense of guilt of a man who feels accused by unknown authorities and feels guilty for not pleasing them; yet these authorities are so beyond his reach that he cannot even learn of what they accuse him, or how he can defend himself. Looked at from this angle, the novel would represent the theological viewpoint most akin to Calvin's theology. Man is condemned or saved without understanding the reasons. All he can do is to tremble and to throw himself upon God's mercy. The theological viewpoint implied in this interpretation is Calvin's concept of guilt, which is representative of the extreme type of authoritarian conscience. However, in one point the authorities in *The Trial* differ fundamentally from Calvin's God. Instead of being glorious and majestic, they are corrupt and dirty. This aspect symbolizes K's rebelliousness toward these authorities. He feels crushed by them and he feels guilty, and yet he hates them and feels their lack of any moral principle. This mixture of submission and rebellion is characteristic of many people who alternately submit and rebel against authorities and particularly against the internalized authority, their conscience.

But K's guilt feeling is simultaneously a reaction of his humanistic conscience. He discovers that he has been "arrested," which means that he has been stopped in his own growth and development. He feels his emptiness and sterility. Kafka in a few sentences masterfully describes the unproductiveness of K's life. This is how he lives:

That spring K had been accustomed to pass his evenings in this way: after work, whenever possible—he was usually in his office until nine—he would take a short walk, alone or with some of his colleagues, and then go to a beer hall, where until eleven he sat at a table patronized mostly by elderly men. But there were exceptions to this routine, when, for instance, the Manager of the Bank, who highly valued his diligence and reliability, invited him for a drive or for dinner at his villa. And once a week K visited a girl called Elsa, who was on duty all night till early morning as a waitress in a cabaret and during the day received her visitors in bed.[42]

K feels guilty without knowing why. He runs away from himself, concerned with finding assistance from others, when only the understanding of the real cause of his guilt feelings and the development of his own productiveness could save him. He asks the inspector who arrests him all kinds of questions about the court and his chances at the trial. He is given the only advice which can be given in this situation. The inspector answers: "However, if I cannot answer your question, I can at least give you a piece of advice. Think less about us and of what is to happen to you; think more about yourself instead."

On another occasion his conscience is represented by the prison chaplain, who shows him that he himself must give account to himself, and that no bribe and no appeal to pity can solve his moral problem. But K can only see the priest as another authority who could intercede for him, and all he is concerned with is whether the priest is angry with him or not. When he tries to appease the priest, the priest shrieks from the pulpit, " 'Can't you see anything at all?' It was an angry cry but at the same time sounded like the involuntary shriek of one who sees another fall and is startled out of himself." But even this shriek does not arouse K. He simply feels more guilty for what he thinks is the priest's anger with him. The priest ends the conversation by saying: " 'So why should I make any claims upon you? The Court makes no claims upon you. It receives you when you come, and it relinquishes you when you go.' " This sentence expresses the essence of humanistic

[42] F. Kafka, *The Trial*, tr. E. I. Muir (New York: Alfred A. Knopf, 1937), p. 23.

conscience. No power transcending man can make
a moral claim upon him. Man is responsible to
himself for gaining or losing his life. Only if he
understands the voice of his conscience, can he
return to himself. If he can not, he will perish;
no one can help him but he himself. K fails to
understand the voice of his conscience, and so he
has to die. At the very moment of the execution,
he has for the first time a glimpse of his real
problem. He senses his own unproductiveness,
his lack of love, and his lack of faith:

> His glance fell on the top storey of the
> house adjoining the quarry. With a flicker as
> of a light going up, the casements of a win-
> dow there suddenly flew open; a human
> figure, faint and insubstantial at that distance
> and that height, leaned abruptly far forward
> and stretched both arms still farther. Who
> was it? A friend? A good man? Someone who
> sympathized? Someone who wanted to help?
> Was it one person only? Or were they all
> there? Was help at hand? Were there some
> arguments in his favour that had been over-
> looked? Of course, there must be. *Logic is
> doubtless unshakable, but it cannot withstand
> a man who wants to go on living.* Where was
> the Judge whom he had never seen? Where
> was the High Court, to which he had never
> penetrated? He raised his hands and spread
> out all his fingers.[43]

For the first time K visualizes the solidarity of
mankind, the possibility of friendship and man's
obligation toward himself. He raises the question
of what the High Court was, but the High Court
about whom he is inquiring now is not the ir-

[43] *Ibid.*, pp. 287-8.

rational authority he had believed in, but the High
Court of his conscience, which is the real accuser
and which he had failed to recognize. K was only
aware of his authoritarian conscience and tried
to manipulate the authorities which it represents.
He was so busy with this activity of self-defense
against someone transcending him that he had
completely lost sight of his real moral problem.
He consciously feels guilty because he is accused
by the authorities, but he *is* guilty because he has
wasted his life and could not change because he
was incapable of understanding his guilt. The
tragedy is that only when it is too late does he have
a vision of what might have been.

It needs to be emphasized that the difference
between humanistic and authoritarian conscience
is not that the latter is molded by the cultural
tradition, while the former develops independently. On the contrary, it is similar in this respect to
our capacities of speech and thought, which,
though intrinsic human potentialities, develop
only in a social and cultural context. The human
race, in the last five or six thousand years of its
cultural development, has formulated ethical
norms in its religious and philosophical systems
toward which the conscience of every individual
must be orientated, if he is not to start from the
beginning. But because of the interests vested in
each system their representatives have tended to
emphasize the differences more than the common
core. Yet, from the standpoint of man, the common elements in these teachings are more important than their differences. If the limitations
and distortions of these teachings are understood
as being the outcome of the particular historical,
socioeconomic, and cultural situation in which
they grew, we find an amazing agreement among
all thinkers whose aim was the growth and happiness of man.

3. Pleasure and Happiness

Happiness is not the reward of virtue, but
is virtue itself; nor do we delight in happiness
because we restrain our lusts; but, on the
contrary, because we delight in it, therefore
are we able to restrain them.

Spinoza, *Ethic*

A. PLEASURE AS A CRITERION OF VALUE

Authoritarian ethics has the advantage of sim-
plicity; its criteria for good or bad are the authority's dicta and to obey them is man's virtue.
Humanistic ethics has to cope with the difficulty
which I have already discussed before: that in
making man the sole judge of values it would seem
that pleasure or pain becomes the final arbiter of
good and evil. If this were the only alternative,
then, indeed, the humanistic principle could not
be the basis for ethical norms. For we see that
some find pleasure in getting drunk, in amassing
wealth, in fame, in hurting people, while others
find pleasure in loving, in sharing things with
friends, in thinking, in painting. How can our life
be guided by a motive by which animal as well
as man, the good and the bad person, the normal
and the sick are motivated alike? Even if we
qualify the pleasure principle by restricting it to
those pleasures which do not injure the legitimate
interests of others, it is hardly adequate as a
guiding principle for our actions.

But this alternative between submission to authority and response to pleasure as guiding principles is fallacious. I shall attempt to show that
an empirical analysis of the nature of pleasure,
satisfaction, happiness, and joy reveals that they
are different and partly contradictory phenomena.
This analysis points to the fact that happiness

and joy although, in a sense, *subjective* experiences, are the outcome of interactions with, and depend on, *objective conditions* and must not be confused with the merely subjective pleasure experience. These objective conditions can be summarized comprehensively as productiveness.

The significance of the qualitative analysis of pleasure has been recognized since the early beginnings of humanistic ethical thinking. The solution of the problem, however, had to remain unsatisfactory inasmuch as insight into the unconscious dynamics of the pleasure experience was lacking. Psychoanalytic research offers new data and suggests new answers to this ancient problem of humanistic ethics. For the better understanding of these findings and their application to ethical theory a brief survey of some of the most important ethical theories on pleasure and happiness seems desirable.

Hedonism maintains that pleasure is the guiding principle of human action, both factually and normatively. Aristippus, the first representative of hedonistic theory, believed the attainment of pleasure and the avoidance of pain to be the aim of life and the criterion of virtue. Pleasure to him is the pleasure of the moment.

This radical—and naïve—hedonistic standpoint had the merit of an uncompromising emphasis on the individual's significance and on a concrete concept of pleasure, making happiness identical with immediate experience.[44] But it was burdened with the obvious difficulty already mentioned, which the hedonists were unable to solve satisfactorily: that of the entirely subjectivistic character of their principle. The first attempt to revise the hedonistic position in introducing *objective*

[44] Cf. H. Marcuse, "Zur Kritik des Hedonismus," *Zschft. f. Sozialforschung*, VII, 1938.

criteria into the concepts of pleasure was made by *Epicurus*, who, though insisting upon pleasure being the aim of life, states that "while every pleasure is in itself good, not all pleasures are to be chosen," since some pleasures cause later annoyances greater than the pleasure itself; according to him, only the *right* pleasure must be conducive to living wisely, well, and righteously. "True" pleasure consists in serenity of mind and the absence of fear, and is obtained only by the man who has prudence and foresight and thus is ready to reject immediate gratification for the sake of permanent and tranquil satisfaction. Epicurus tries to show that his concept of pleasure as the aim of life is consistent with the virtues of temperance, courage, justice, and friendship. But using *"feeling* as the canon by which we judge every good," he did not overcome the basic theoretical difficulty: that of combining the subjective experience of pleasure with the objective criterion of "right" and "wrong" pleasure. His attempt to harmonize subjective and objective criteria did not go beyond the *assertion* that the harmony existed.

Nonhedonistic humanistic philosophers coped with the same problem, attempting to preserve the criteria of truth and universality, yet not to lose sight of the happiness of the individual as the ultimate goal of life.

The first to apply the criterion of truth and falsehood to desires and pleasures was *Plato*. Pleasure, like thought, can be *true* or *false*. Plato does not deny the reality of the subjective sensation of pleasure, but he points out that the pleasure sensation can be "mistaken" and that pleasure has a *cognitive* function like thinking. Plato supports this view with the theory that pleasure springs not only from an isolated, sensuous part of a person but from the total personality. Hence he concludes that *good men have true pleasures; bad men, false pleasures.*

Aristotle, like Plato, maintains that the subjective experience of pleasure can not be a criterion for the goodness of the activity and, thereby, of its value. He says that "if things are pleasant to people of vicious constitution, we must not suppose that they are also pleasant to others than these, just as we do not reason so about the things that are wholesome or sweet or bitter to sick people, or ascribe whiteness to the things that seem white to those suffering from a disease of the eye."[45] Disgraceful pleasures are not really pleasures, "except to a perverted taste," while the pleasures which objectively deserve this name accompany those "activities which are proper to man."[46] For Aristotle, there are two legitimate kinds of pleasure, those which are associated with the *process* of fulfilling needs and realizing our powers; and those which are associated with the *exercise* of our powers when acquired. The latter is the superior kind of pleasure. Pleasure is an activity (energia) of the natural state of one's being. The most satisfactory and complete pleasure is a quality supervening on the active use of acquired or realized powers. It implies joy and spontaneity, or unimpeded activity, where "unimpeded" means "not blocked" or "frustrated." Thus pleasure perfects activities and hence perfects life. Pleasure and life are joined together and do not admit of separation. The greatest and most enduring happiness results from the highest human activity, which is akin to the divine, that of the activity of reason, and in so far as man has a divine element in him he will pursue such an activity.[47] Aristotle thus arrives at a concept

---

[45] Aristotle, *Ethics*, 1173, 21 ff.
[46] Aristotle, *Ethics*, 1176ᵃ, 15–30.
[47] See Book VII, Chaps. 11–13, and Book X, Chaps. 4, 7, 8.

of *true* pleasure which is identical with subjective pleasure experience of the healthy and mature person.

Spinoza's theory of pleasure is similar, in certain aspects, to Plato's and Aristotle's; but he goes far beyond them. He, too, believed that joy is a result of right or virtuous living and not an indication of sinfulness, as the antipleasure schools maintain. He furthered the theory by giving a more empirical and specific definition of joy which was based upon his whole anthropological concept. Spinoza's concept of joy is related to that of potency (power). "Joy is a man's passage from a less to a greater perfection; sorrow is a man's passage from a greater to a less perfection."[48] Greater or lesser perfection is the same as greater or lesser power to realize one's potentialities and thus to approach more closely "the model of human nature." Pleasure is not the *aim* of life but it inevitably accompanies man's productive activity. "Blessedness (or happiness) is not the reward of virtue but virtue itself."[49] The significance of Spinoza's view on happiness lies in his dynamic concept of power. Goethe, Guyau, Nietzsche, to name only some important names, have built their ethical theories on the same thought—that pleasure is not a primary motive of action but a companion of productive activity.

In *Spencer's Ethics* we find one of the most comprehensive and systematic discussions of the pleasure principle, which we can use as an excellent starting point for further discussion.

The key to Spencer's view of the pleasure-pain principle is the concept of evolution. He proposes that pleasure and pain have the biological function of stimulating man to act according to what is beneficial to him individually as well as to the

---

[48] *Ethics*, III, Re Affects, Def. II, III.
[49] *Ibid.*, Prop. XLII.

human race; they are therefore indispensable factors in the evolutionary process. "Pains are the correlatives of actions injurious to the organism, while pleasures are correlatives of actions conducive to its welfare."[50] "Individual or species is from day to day kept alive by pursuit of the agreeable or avoidance of the disagreeable."[51] Pleasure, while being a subjective experience, can not be judged in terms of the subjective element alone; it has an objective aspect, namely, that of man's physical and mental welfare. Spencer admits that in our present culture many cases of "perverted" pleasure or pain experience occur, and he explains this phenomenon by the contradictions and imperfections of society. He claims that "with complete adjustment of humanity to the social state, will go recognition of the truths that actions are completely right only when, besides being conducive to future happiness, special and general, they are immediately pleasurable, and that painfulness, not ultimate but proximate, is the concomitant of actions which are wrong."[52] He said that those who believe that pain has a beneficial or pleasure a detrimental effect are guilty of a distortion which makes the exception appear to be the rule.

Spencer parallels his theory of the biological function of pleasure with a sociological theory. He proposes that "remoulding of human nature into fitness for the requirements of social life must eventually make *all* needful activities pleasurable, while it makes displeasurable activities at variance with these requirements."[53] And further "that the pleasure attending on the use of means to achieve an end, itself becomes an end."[54]

---

[50] H. Spencer, *The Principles of Ethics* (New York: D. Appleton Co., 1902), Vol. I.

[51] *Ibid.*, pp. 79, 82.

[52] *Ibid.*, p. 99.

[53] *Ibid.*, p. 183.

[54] *Ibid.*, p. 159.

The concepts of Plato, Aristotle, Spinoza, and Spencer have in common the ideas (1) that the subjective experience of pleasure is in itself not a sufficient criterion of *value;* (2) that happiness is conjunctive with the good; (3) that an objective criterion for the evaluation of pleasure can be found. Plato referred to the "good man" as the criterion of the right pleasure; Aristotle, to "the function of man"; Spinoza, like Aristotle, to the realization of man's nature by the use of his powers; Spencer, to the biological and social evolution of man.

The foregoing theories of pleasure and its role in ethics suffered from the fact that they were not constructed from sufficiently refined data based on precise techniques of study and observation. Psychoanalysis, in its minute study of unconscious motivations and of the dynamics of character, laid the foundation for such refined techniques of study and observation and thus enables us to further the discussion of pleasure as a norm for living beyond its traditional scope.

Psychoanalysis confirms the view, held by the opponents of hedonistic ethics, that the subjective experience of satisfaction is in itself deceptive and not a valid criterion of value. The psychoanalytic insight into the nature of masochistic strivings confirms the correctness of the antihedonistic position. All masochistic desires can be described as a *craving for that which is harmful* to the total personality. In its more obvious forms, masochism is the striving for physical pain and the subsequent enjoyment of that pain. As a perversion, masochism is related to sexual excitement and satisfaction, the desire for pain being conscious. "Moral masochism" is the striving for being harmed psychically, humiliated, and dominated; usually this wish is not conscious, but it is rationalized as loyalty, love, or self-negation, or as a response to the laws of nature, to fate, or to other powers transcending man. Psychoanalysis shows how deeply repressed and how well rationalized the masochistic striving can be.

The masochistic phenomena, however, are only a particularly striking instance of unconscious desires which are objectively harmful; all neuroses can be understood as the result of unconscious strivings which tend to harm and to block a person's growth. To crave that which is harmful is the very essence of mental sickness. Every neurosis thus confirms the fact that pleasure can be in contradiction to man's real interests.

The pleasure arising from the satisfaction of neurotic cravings can be, but is not necessarily, unconscious. The masochistic perversion is an example of conscious pleasure from a neurotic craving. The sadistic person getting satisfaction from humiliating people, or the miser enjoying the money he hoarded, may or may not be aware of the pleasure he derives from the satisfaction of his craving. Whether or not such pleasure is conscious or repressed depends on two factors: on the strength of those forces within a person opposing his irrational strivings; and on the degree to which the mores of society sanction or outlaw the enjoyment of such pleasure. Repression of pleasure can have two different meanings; the less thorough and more frequent form of repression is the one in which pleasure is felt consciously but not in connection with the irrational striving as such, but rather with a rationalized expression of it. The miser, for instance, may think he feels satisfaction because of his prudent care for his family; the sadist may feel that his pleasure is derived from his sense of moral indignation. The more radical type of repression is that in which there is no awareness of any pleasure. Many a sadistic person will deny sincerely that the experience of seeing others humiliated gives him any feeling of pleasure. Yet the analysis of his dreams and free associations uncovers the existence of unconscious pleasure.

Pain and unhappiness can also be unconscious and the repression can assume the same forms just described with regard to pleasure. A person may feel unhappy because he does not have as much success as he desires, or because his health is impaired, or because of any number of external circumstances in his life; the fundamental reason for his unhappiness, however, may be his lack of productiveness, the emptiness of his life, his incapacity to love, or any number of *inner* defects which make him unhappy. He rationalizes his unhappiness, as it were, and thus does not feel it in connection with its real cause. Again, the more thorough kind of repression of unhappiness occurs where there is no consciousness of unhappiness at all. In this case a person believes he is perfectly happy, while actually he is discontented and unhappy.

The concept of unconscious happiness and unhappiness meets with an important objection which says that happiness and unhappiness are identical with our conscious feeling of being happy or unhappy and that to be pleased or pained without knowing it is equivalent to not being pleased or pained. This argument has more than merely theoretical significance. It is of utmost importance in its social and ethical implications. If slaves are not aware of being pained by their lot, how can the outsider object to slavery in the name of man's happiness? If modern man is as happy as he pretends to be, does this not prove that we have built the best of all possible worlds? Is the illusion of happiness not sufficient or, rather is "illusion of happiness" not a self-contradictory concept?

These objections ignore the fact that happiness as well as unhappiness is more than a state of mind. In fact, happiness and unhappiness are expressions of the state of the entire organism, of the total personality. Happiness is conjunctive with an increase in vitality, intensity of feeling and thinking, and productiveness; unhappiness is conjunctive with the decrease of these capacities and functions. Happiness and unhappiness are so much a state of our total personality that bodily reactions are frequently more expressive of them than our conscious feeling. The drawn face of a person, listlessness, tiredness, or physical symptoms like headaches or even more serious forms of illness are frequent expressions of unhappiness, just as a physical feeling of well-being can be one of the "symptoms" of happiness. Indeed, our body is less capable of being deceived about the state of happiness than our mind, and one can entertain the idea that some time in the future the presence and degree of happiness and unhappiness might be inferred from an examination of the chemical processes in the body. Likewise, the functioning of our mental and emotional capacities is influenced by our happiness or unhappiness. The acuteness of our reason and the intensity of our feelings depend on it. Unhappiness weakens or even paralyzes all our psychic functions. Happiness increases them. The subjective feeling of being happy, when it is not a quality of the state of well-being of the whole person, is nothing more than an illusory thought *about* a feeling and is completely unrelated to genuine happiness.

Pleasure or happiness which exists only in a person's head but is not a condition of his personality I propose to call pseudo-pleasure or pseudo-happiness. A person, for instance, takes a trip and is consciously happy; yet he may have this feeling because happiness is what he is supposed to experience on a pleasure trip; actually, he may be unconsciously disappointed and unhappy. A dream may reveal the truth to him; or perhaps, he will realize later that his happiness was not genuine. Pseudo-pain can be observed in many situations in which sorrow or unhappiness are conventionally expected and therefore felt. Pseudo-pleasure and pseudo-pain are actually only pretended feelings; they are *thoughts about feelings*, rather than genuine emotional experiences.

B. TYPES OF PLEASURE

The analysis of the qualitative difference between the various kinds of pleasure is, as already indicated, the key to the problem of the relation between pleasure and ethical values.[55]

One type of pleasure which Freud and others thought was the essence of all pleasure is the feeling accompanying the *relief from painful tension*. Hunger, thirst, and the need for sexual satisfaction, sleep, and bodily exercise are rooted in the chemism of the organism. The objective, physiological necessity to satisfy these demands is perceived subjectively as desire, and if they remain unsatisfied for any length of time painful tension is felt. If this tension is released, the relief is felt as pleasure or, as I propose to call it, *satisfaction*. This term, from *satis-facere* = to make sufficient, seems to be most appropriate for this kind of pleasure. It is the very nature of all such physiologically conditioned needs that their satisfaction ends the tension due to the physiological changes brought about in the organism. If we are hungry and eat, our organism—and we—have enough at a certain point beyond which further eating would actually be painful. The satisfaction in relieving painful tension is the most common

---

[55] It does not seem to be necessary nowadays to show the fallacy of Bentham's assumption that all pleasures are qualitatively alike and only different in quantity. Hardly any psychologist holds this view any more, even though the popular idea of "having fun" still implies that all pleasures have the same quality.

pleasure and the easiest to obtain psychologically; it can also be one of the most intense pleasures if the tension has lasted long enough and therefore has become sufficiently intense itself. The significance of this type of pleasure cannot be doubted; nor can it be doubted that it constitutes in the lives of not a few almost the only form of pleasure they ever experience.

A type of pleasure also caused by relief from tension, but different in quality from the one described, is rooted in psychic tension. A person may feel that a desire is due to the demands of his body, while actually it is determined by irrational psychic needs. He can have intense hunger which is not caused by the normal, physiologically conditioned need of his organism but by *psychic* needs to allay anxiety or depression (although these may be concomitant with abnormal physiochemical processes). It is well known that the need for drinking is often not due to thirst but is psychically conditioned.

Intense sexual desire, too, can be caused not by physiological but by psychic needs. An insecure person who has an intense need to prove his worth to himself, to show others how irresistible he is, or to dominate others by "making" them sexually, will easily feel intense sexual desires, and a painful tension if the desires are not satisfied. He will be prone to think that the intensity of his desires is due to the demands of his body, while actually these demands are determined by his psychic needs. Neurotic sleepiness is another example of a desire which is felt to be caused by bodily conditions like normal tiredness, although it is actually caused by psychic conditions such as repressed anxiety, fear, or anger.

These desires are similar to the normal, physiologically conditioned needs inasmuch as both are rooted in a lack or in a deficiency. In the one case the deficiency is grounded in normal chemical processes within the organism; in the other case it is the result of psychic dysfunctioning. In both cases the deficiency causes tensions and the relief from it results in pleasure. All other irrational desires which do not assume the form of bodily needs, like the passionate craving for fame, for domination, or for submission, envy, and jealousy, are also rooted in the character structure of a person and spring from a crippling or distortion within the personality. The pleasure felt in the satisfaction of these passions is also caused by the relief from psychic tension as in the case of neurotically conditioned bodily desires.

Although the pleasure derived from the satisfaction of genuine physiological needs and of irrational psychic needs consists in the relief from tension, the quality of the pleasure differs significantly. The physiologically conditioned desires such as hunger, thirst, and so on, are satisfied with the removal of the physiologically conditioned tension, and they reappear only when the physiological need arises again; they are thus rhythmic in nature. The irrational desires, in contrast, are insatiable. The desire of the envious, the possessive, the sadistic person does not disappear with its satisfaction, except perhaps momentarily. It is in the very nature of these irrational desires that they can not be "satisfied." They spring from a dissatisfaction within oneself. The lack of productiveness and the resulting powerlessness and fear are the root of these passionate cravings and irrational desires. Even if man could satisfy all his wishes for power and destruction, it would not change his fear and loneliness, and thus the tension would remain. The blessing of imagination turns into a curse; since a person does not find himself relieved from his fears, he imagines ever-increasing satisfactions would cure his greed and restore his inner balance. But greed is a bottomless pit, and the idea of the relief derived from its satisfaction is a mirage. Greed, indeed, is not, as is so often assumed, rooted in man's animal nature but in his mind and imagination.

We have seen that the pleasures derived from the fulfillment of physiological needs and neurotic desires are the result of the removal of painful tension. But while those in the first category are really satisfying, are normal, and are a condition for happiness, those in the latter are at best only a temporary mitigation of need, an indication of pathological functioning and of fundamental unhappiness. I propose to call the pleasure derived from the fulfillment of irrational desires "irrational pleasure" in contradistinction to "satisfaction," which is the fulfillment of normal physiological desires.

For the problem of ethics, the difference between irrational pleasure and happiness is much more important than that between irrational pleasure and satisfaction. In order to understand these distinctions, it may be helpful to introduce the concept of psychological *scarcity* versus *abundance*.

The unfulfilled needs of the body create tension, the removal of which gives satisfaction. The very lack is the basis of the satisfaction. In a different sense, irrational desires are also rooted in deficiencies, in a person's insecurity and anxiety, which compel him to hate, to envy, or to submit; the pleasure derived from the fulfillment of these cravings is rooted in the fundamental lack of productiveness. Both physiological and irrational psychic needs are part of a system of scarcity.

But beyond the realm of scarcity rises the realm of *abundance*. While even in the animal, surplus energy is present and is expressed in play,[56] the realm of abundance is essentially a human phe-

---

[56] This problem has been analyzed in G. Bally's excellent study, *Vom Ursprung und von den Grenzen der Freiheit* (B. Schwabe Co., Basel, 1945).

nomenon. It is the realm of productiveness, of inner activity. This realm can exist only to the extent to which man does not have to work for sheer subsistence and thus to use up most of his energy. The evolution of the human race is characterized by the expansion of the realm of abundance, of the surplus energy available for achievements beyond mere survival. All specifically *human* achievements of man spring from abundance.

In all spheres of activity the difference between scarcity and abundance and therefore between satisfaction and happiness exists, even with regard to elementary functions like hunger and sex. To satisfy the physiological need of intense hunger is pleasureful because it relieves tension. Different in quality from satisfaction of hunger is the pleasure derived from the satisfaction of appetite. Appetite is the anticipation of enjoyable taste experience and, in distinction to hunger, does not produce tension. Taste in this sense is a product of cultural development and refinement like musical or artistic taste and can develop only in a situation of abundance, both in the cultural and the psychological meaning of the word. Hunger is a phenomenon of scarcity; its satisfaction, a necessity. Appetite is a phenomenon of abundance; its satisfaction not a necessity but an expression of freedom and productiveness. The pleasure accompanying it may be called joy.[57]

With regard to sex a distinction similar to that between hunger and appetite can be made. Freud's

[57] Since at this point I want to make clear only the difference between scarcity-pleasure and abundance-pleasure, I hardly need to go into further details of the hunger-appetite problem. Suffice it to say that in appetite a genuine amount of hunger is always present. The physiological basis of the eating function affects us in such a way that complete absence of hunger would also diminish appetite to a minimum. What matters, however, is the respective weight of the motivation.

concept of sex is that of an urge springing entirely from physiologically conditioned tension, relieved, like hunger, by satisfaction. But he ignores sexual desire and pleasure corresponding to appetite, which only can exist in the realm of abundance and which is exclusively a human phenomenon. The sexually "hungry" person is satisfied by the relief from tension, either physiological or psychic, and this satisfaction constitutes his pleasure.[58] But sexual pleasure which we call joy is rooted in abundance and freedom and is the expression of sensual and emotional productiveness.

Joy and happiness are widely believed to be identical with the happiness accompanying love. In fact, to many, love is supposed to be the only source of happiness. Yet, in love as in all other human activities, we must differentiate between the productive and the nonproductive form. Nonproductive or irrational love can be, as I have shown before, any kind of masochistic or sadistic symbiosis, where the relationship is not based upon mutual respect and integrity but where two persons depend on each other because they are incapable of depending on themselves. This love, like all other irrational strivings, is based on scarcity, on the lack of productiveness and inner security. Productive love, the closest form of relatedness between two people and simultaneously one in which the integrity of each is preserved, is a phenomenon of abundance, and the ability for it is the testimony to human maturity. Joy and happiness are the concomitants of productive love.

In all spheres of activity the difference between scarcity and abundance determines the quality of the pleasure experience. Every person experi-

---

[58] The classic saying, *"Omne animal triste post coitum"* ("All animals are sad after intercourse"), is an adequate description of sexual satisfaction on the level of scarcity as far as human beings are concerned.

ences satisfactions, irrational pleasures, and joy. What distinguishes people is the respective weight of each of these pleasures in their lives. Satisfaction and irrational pleasure do not require an emotional effort; only the ability to produce the conditions relieving the tension. Joy is an achievement; it presupposes an inner effort, that of productive activity.

Happiness is an achievement brought about by man's inner productiveness and not a gift of the gods. Happiness and joy are not the satisfaction of a need springing from a physiological or a psychological lack; they are not the relief from tension but the accompaniment of all productive activity, in thought, feeling, and action. Joy and happiness are not different in quality; they are different only inasmuch as joy refers to a single act while happiness may be said to be a continuous or integrated experience of joy; we can speak of "joys" (in the plural) but only of "happiness" (in the singular).

Happiness is the indication that man has found the answer to the problem of human existence: the productive realization of his potentialities and thus, simultaneously, being one with the world and preserving the integrity of his self. In spending his energy productively he increases his powers, he "burns without being consumed."

Happiness is the criterion of excellence in the art of living, of virtue in the meaning it has in humanistic ethics. Happiness is often considered the logical opposite of grief or pain. Physical or mental suffering is part of human existence and to experience them is unavoidable. To spare oneself from grief at all cost can be achieved only at the price of total detachment, which excludes the ability to experience happiness. The opposite of happiness thus is not grief or pain but depression which results from inner sterility and unproductiveness.

We have dealt so far with the types of pleasure experience most relevant to ethical theory: satisfaction, irrational pleasure, joy, and happiness. It remains to consider briefly two other less complex types of pleasure. One is the pleasure which accompanies the accomplishment of any kind of task one has set out to do. I propose to call this kind of pleasure "gratification." Having achieved something which one wanted to accomplish is gratifying although the activity is not necessarily productive; but it is a proof of one's power and ability to cope successfully with the outside world. Gratification does not depend very much on a specific activity; a man may find as much gratification in a good game of tennis as in success in business; what matters is that there is some difficulty in the task he has set out to accomplish and that he has achieved a satisfactory result.

The other type of pleasure which is left for discussion is not based on effort but on its opposite, on relaxation; it accompanies effortless but pleasant activities. The important biological function of relaxation is that of regulating the rhythm of the organism, which cannot be always active. The word "pleasure," without qualification, seems to be most appropriate to denote the kind of good feeling that results from relaxation.

We started out with the discussion of the problematic character of hedonistic ethics, which claims that the *aim* of life *is* pleasure and that therefore pleasure is good in itself. As a result of our analysis of the various kinds of pleasure we are now in a position to formulate our view on the ethical relevance of pleasure. Satisfaction as relief from physiologically conditioned tension is neither good nor bad; as far as ethical evaluation is concerned it is ethically neutral, as are gratification and pleasure. Irrational pleasure and happiness (joy) are experiences of ethical significance. Irrational pleasure is the indication of greed, of the failure to solve the problem of human existence. Happiness (joy), on the contrary, is proof of partial or total success in the "art of living." Happiness is man's greatest achievement; it is the response of his total personality to a productive orientation toward himself and the world outside.

Hedonistic thinking failed to analyze the nature of pleasure sufficiently; it thus made it appear as if that which is easiest in life—to have *some* kind of pleasure—were at the same time that which is most valuable. But nothing valuable is easy; thus the hedonistic error made it easier to argue against freedom and happiness and to maintain that the very denial of pleasure was a proof of goodness. Humanistic ethics may very well postulate happiness and joy as its chief virtues, but in doing so it does not demand the easiest but *the most difficult task of man, the full development of his productiveness.*

C. THE PROBLEM OF MEANS AND ENDS

The problem of the pleasure in ends as against the pleasure in means is of particular significance for contemporary society, in which the ends have often been forgotten in an obsessive concern with the means.

The problem of ends and means has been formulated by Spencer very clearly. He proposed that pleasure connected with an end *necessarily* makes the means to this end also pleasureful. He assumes that in a state of complete adjustment of humanity to the social state, "actions are completely right only when, besides being conducive to future happiness, special or general, they are immediately pleasurable, or that painfulness, not only ultimate but proximate, is the concomitant of actions which are wrong."[59]

---

[59] *Principles of Ethics*, Vol. I, p. 49.

At first glance Spencer's assumption seems plausible. If a person plans a pleasure trip, for instance, the preparations for it may be pleasureful; but it is obvious that this is not always true and that there are many acts preparatory to a desired end which are not pleasureful. If a sick person has to endure a painful treatment, the end-in-view, his health, does not make the treatment itself pleasureful; nor do the pains of childbirth become pleasureful. In order to achieve a desired end we do many unpleasant things only because our *reason* tells us that we have to do them. At best, it can be said that the unpleasantness may be more or less diminished by the anticipation of the pleasure in the result; the anticipation of the end-pleasure may even outweigh completely the discomfort connected with the means.

But the importance of the problem of means and ends does not end here. More significant are aspects of the problem which can be understood only by considering unconscious motivations.

We can make good use of an illustration for the means-ends relationship which Spencer offers. He describes the pleasure which a businessman derives from the fact that when his books are balanced from time to time the result proves correct to a penny. "If you ask," he says, "why all this elaborate process, so remote from the actual making of money and still more remote from the enjoyments of life, the answer is that keeping accounts correctly is fulfilling a condition to the end of money making, and becomes in itself a proximate end—a duty to be discharged—that there may be discharged the duty of getting an income, that there may be discharged the duty of maintaining self, wife, and children."[60] In Spencer's view, the pleasure in the means, bookkeeping, is derived from the pleasure in the end:

[60] *Ibid.*, p. 161.

enjoyment of life, or "duty." Spencer failed to recognize two problems. The more obvious one is that the *consciously* perceived end may be something different from the one which is perceived *unconsciously*. A person may *think* that his aim (or his motive) is the enjoyment of life or the fulfillment of duty toward his family, while his real, though unconscious, aim is the power he attains through money or the pleasure derived from hoarding it.

The second—and more important—problem arises from the assumption that the pleasure connected with the means is necessarily derived from the pleasure connected with the end. While it *may* happen, of course, that the pleasure in the end, the future use of the money, makes the means to this end (bookkeeping) also pleasureful, as Spencer assumes, the pleasure in bookkeeping may be derived from an entirely different source and its connection with the end may be fictitious. A case in point would be an obsessional businessman who enjoys his bookkeeping activities tremendously and is greatly pleased when his accounts prove to be correct to the penny. If we examine his pleasure we will find that he is a person filled with anxiety and doubt; he enjoys bookkeeping because he is "active" without having to make decisions or take risks. If the books balance he is pleased because the correctness of his figures is a symbolic answer to his doubts about himself and about life. Bookkeeping to him has the same function as playing solitaire may have for another person or counting the windows of a house to still another. *The means have become independent of the aim;* they have usurped the role of the end, and *the alleged aim exists only in imagination.*

The most outstanding example—relative to Spencer's illustration—of a means which has made itself independent and has become pleasureful, not because of the pleasure in the end but because of factors completely divorced from it, is the meaning of work as it developed in the centuries following the Reformation, especially under the influence of Calvinism.

The problem under discussion touches upon one of the sorest spots of contemporary society. One of the most outstanding psychological features of modern life is the fact that activities which are means to ends have more and more usurped the position of ends, while the ends themselves have a shadowy and unreal existence. People work in order to make money; they make money in order to do enjoyable things with it. The work is the means, the enjoyment, the end. But what happens actually? People work in order to make more money; they use this money in order to make still more money, and the end—the enjoyment of life —is lost sight of. People are in a hurry and invent things in order to have more time. Then they use the time saved to rush about again to save more time until they are so exhausted that they can not use the time they saved. We have become enmeshed in a net of means and have lost sight of ends. We have radios which can bring to everybody the best in music and literature. What we hear instead is, to a large extent, trash at the pulp magazine level or advertising which is an insult to intelligence and taste. We have the most wonderful instruments and means man has ever had, but we do not stop and ask *what they are for.*[61]

The overemphasis on ends leads to a distortion of the harmonious balance between means and ends in various ways: one way is that all emphasis is on *ends* without sufficient consideration of the role of means. The outcome of this distortion is that ends become abstract, unreal, and eventually

---

[61] A. de Saint-Exupéry, in his *Little Prince*, has given an excellent description of this very pattern. (New York: Reynal and Hitchcock, 1943.)

nothing but pipe dreams. This danger has been discussed at length by Dewey. The isolation of ends can have the opposite effect: while the end is ideologically retained it serves merely as a cover for shifting all the emphasis to those activities which are allegedly means to this end. The motto for this mechanism is "The ends justify the means." The defenders of this principle fail to see that the use of destructive means has its own consequences which actually *transform* the end even if it is still retained ideologically.

Spencer's concept of the social function of pleasurable activities has an important *sociological* bearing on the means-ends problem. In connection with his view that the pleasure experience has the biological function of making activities which are conducive to human welfare pleasant, and thereby attractive, he states that "remoulding of human nature into fitness for the requirement of social life, must eventually make all needful activities pleasurable, while it makes displeasurable all activities at variance with these requirements."[62] He continues that "supposing it consistent with the maintenance of life, there is no kind of activity which will not become a source of pleasure, if continued, and that therefore pleasure will eventually accompany every move or action demanded by social conditions."[63]

Spencer touches here upon one of the most significant mechanisms of society: that any given society tends to form the character-structure of its members in such a way as *to make them desire to do what they have to do in order to fulfill their social function.* But he fails to see that, in a society detrimental to the *real* human interest of its members, activities which are harmful to man but useful to the functioning of that particular

---

[62] *Principles of Ethics*, Vol. I, p. 138.
[63] *Ibid.*, p. 186.

society can also become sources of satisfaction. Even slaves have learned to be satisfied with their lot; oppressors, to enjoy cruelty. The cohesion of every society rests upon the very fact that there is almost no activity which can not be made pleasureful, a fact which suggests that the phenomenon that Spencer describes can be a source of blocking as well as of furthering social progress. What matters is the understanding of the meaning and function of any particular activity and of the satisfaction derived from it in terms of the nature of man and of the proper conditions for his life. As has been pointed out above, the satisfaction derived from irrational strivings differs in kind from the pleasure derived from activities conducive to human welfare, and such satisfaction is not a criterion of value. Just because Spencer is right in proposing that every socially useful activity *can* become a source of pleasure, he is wrong in assuming that therefore the pleasure connected with such activities proves their moral value. Only by analyzing the nature of man and by uncovering the very contradictions between his *real* interests and those *imposed* upon him by a given society, can one arrive at the objectively valid norms which Spencer strove to discover. His optimism with regard to his own society and its future, and his lack of a psychology which dealt with the phenomenon of irrational cravings and their satisfaction, caused him unwittingly to pave the way for the relativism in ethics which today has become so popular.

4. Faith as a Character Trait

> Belief consists in accepting the affirmations
> of the soul; unbelief in denying them.
> —Emerson

Faith is not one of the concepts that fits into the intellectual climate of the present-day world. One usually associates faith with God and with religious doctrines, in contradistinction to rational and scientific thinking. The latter is assumed to refer to the realm of facts, distinguished from a realm transcending facts where scientific thinking has no place, and only faith rules. To many, this division is untenable. If faith can not be reconciled with rational thinking, it has to be eliminated as an anachronistic remnant of earlier stages of culture and replaced by science dealing with facts and theories which are intelligible and can be validated.

The modern attitude toward faith was reached after a long drawn-out struggle against the authority of the church and its claim to control any kind of thinking. Thus skepticism with regard to faith is bound up with the very advance of reason. This constructive side of modern skepticism, however, has a reverse side which has been neglected.

Insight into the character structure of modern man and the contemporary social scene leads to the realization that the current widespread lack of faith no longer has the progressive aspect it had generations ago. Then the fight against faith was a fight for emancipation from spiritual shackles; it was a fight against irrational belief, the expression of faith in man's reason and his ability to establish a social order governed by the principles of freedom, equality, and brotherliness. Today the lack of faith is the expression of profound con-

fusion and despair. Once skepticism and rationalism were progressive forces for the development
of thought; now they have become rationalizations
for relativism and uncertainty. The belief that the
gathering of more and more facts will inevitably
result in knowing the truth has become a superstition. Truth itself is looked upon, in certain quar-
ters, as a metaphysical concept, and science as
restricted to the task of gathering information.
Behind a front of alleged rational certainty, there
is a profound uncertainty which makes people
ready to accept or to compromise with any philosophy impressed upon them.

Can man live without faith? Must not the nurs-
ling have "faith in his mother's breast"? Must
we all not have faith in our fellow men, in those
whom we love and in ourselves? Can we live without faith in the validity of norms for our life?
Indeed, without faith man becomes sterile, hope-
less, and afraid to the very core of his being.

Was, then, the fight against faith idle, and were
the achievements of reason ineffectual? Must we
return to religion or resign ourselves to live without faith? Is faith necessarily a matter of belief
in God or in religious doctrines? Is it linked so
closely with religion as to have to share its des-
tiny? Is faith by necessity in contrast to, or
divorced from, rational thinking? I shall attempt
to show that these questions can be answered by
considering faith to be a basic *attitude* of a person,
a character trait which pervades all his experiences, which enables a man to face reality without
illusions and yet to live by his faith. It is difficult
to think of faith not primarily as faith *in* something, but of faith as an inner attitude the specific
object of which is of secondary importance. It may
be helpful to remember that the term "faith" as
it is used in the Old Testament—"Emunah"—
means "firmness" and thereby denotes a certain
quality of human experience, a character trait,

rather than the content of a belief in something.

For the understanding of this problem it may be helpful to approach it by first discussing the problem of doubt. Doubt, too, is usually understood as doubt or perplexity concerning this or that assumption, idea, or person, but it can also be described as an *attitude* which permeates one's personality, so that the particular object on which one fastens one's doubt is of but secondary importance. In order to understand the phenomenon of doubt, one must differentiate between *rational* and *irrational* doubt. I shall presently make this same discrimination with regard to the phenomenon of faith.

Irrational doubt is not the intellectual reaction to an improper or plainly mistaken assumption, but rather the doubt which colors a person's life emotionally and intellectually. To him, there is no experience in any sphere of life which has the quality of certainty; everything is doubtful, nothing is certain.

The most extreme form of irrational doubt is the neurotic compulsion to doubt. The person beset by it is compulsively driven to doubt everything he thinks about or to be perplexed by everything he does. The doubt often refers to the most important questions and decisions in life. It often intrudes upon trifling decisions, such as which suit to wear or whether or not to go to a party. Regardless of the objects of the doubt, whether they are trifling or important, irrational doubt is agonizing and exhausting.

The psychoanalytic inquiry into the mechanism of compulsive doubts shows that they are the rationalized expression of unconscious emotional conflicts, resulting from a lack of integration of the total personality and from an intense feeling of powerlessness and helplessness. Only by recognizing the roots of the doubt can one overcome the paralysis of will which springs from the inner ex-

perience of powerlessness. When such insight has
not been attained, substitute solutions are found
which, while unsatisfactory, at least do away with
the tormenting manifest doubts. One of these
substitutes is compulsive activity in which the
person is able to find temporary relief. Another
is the acceptance of some "faith" in which a person, as it were, submerges himself and his doubts.

The typical form of contemporary doubt, however, is not the active one described above but
rather an attitude of *indifference* in which *everything is possible, nothing is certain*. An increasing
number of people are feeling confused about
everything, work, politics, and morals and, what
is worse, they believe this very confusion to be
a normal state of mind. They feel isolated, bewildered, and powerless; they do not experience
life in terms of their own thoughts, emotions, and
sense perceptions, but in terms of the experiences
they are supposed to have. Although in these auto-
matized persons active doubt has disappeared,
indifference and relativism have taken its place.

In contrast to irrational doubt, *rational doubt*
questions assumptions the validity of which depends on belief in an authority and not on one's
own experience. This doubt has an important
function in personality development. The child
at first accepts all ideas on the unquestioned authority of his parents. In the process of emancipat-
ing himself from their authority, in developing his
own self, he becomes critical. In the process of
growing up, the child starts to doubt the legends
he previously accepted without question, and the
increase of his critical capacities is directly proportionate to his becoming independent of parental authority and to his becoming an adult.

Historically, rational doubt is one of the main-
springs of modern thought, and through it modern
philosophy, as well as science, received their most
fruitful impulses. Here too, as in personal de-

velopment, the rise of rational doubt was linked with the growing emancipation from authority, that of the church and the state.

In regard to *faith*, I wish to make the same differentiation which was made with regard to doubt: that between irrational and rational faith. By irrational faith I understand the belief in a person, idea, or symbol which does not result from one's own experience of thought or feeling, but which is based on one's emotional submission to irrational authority.

Before we go on, the connection between submission and intellectual and emotional processes must be explored further. There is ample evidence that a person who has given up his inner independence and submitted to an authority tends to substitute the authority's experience for his own. The most impressive illustration is to be found in the hypnotic situation where a person surrenders to the authority of another and, in the state of hypnotic sleep, is ready to think and feel what the hypnotist "makes him" think and feel. Even after he has awakened from the hypnotic sleep he will follow suggestions given by the hypnotist, though thinking that he is following his own judgment and initiative. If the hypnotist, for instance, has given the suggestion that at a certain hour the subject will feel cold and should put on his coat, he will in the posthypnotic situation have the suggested feeling and will act accordingly, being convinced that his feelings and acts are based on reality and initiated by his own conviction and will.

While the hypnotic situation is the most conclusive experiment in demonstrating the interrelation between submission to an authority and thought processes, there are many relatively commonplace situations revealing the same mechanism. The reaction of people to a leader equipped with a strong power of suggestion is an example

of a semi-hypnotic situation. Here too the unqualified acceptance of his ideas is not rooted
in the listeners' conviction based upon their own
thinking or their critical appraisal of the ideas
presented to them, but instead in their emotional
submission to the speaker. People in this situation
have the illusion that they agree, that they
rationally approve of the ideas the speaker suggested. They feel that they accept him because
they agree with his ideas. In reality the sequence
is the opposite: they accept his ideas because they
have submitted to his authority in a semihypnotic
fashion. Hitler gave a good description of this
process in his discussion of the advisability of
holding propaganda meetings at night. He said
that the "superior oratorical talent of a domineer-
ing apostolic nature will now [in the evening]
succeed more easily in winning for the new will
people who themselves have in turn experienced
a weakening of their force of resistance in the
most natural way than people who still have full
command of their energies and their will power."[64]

For irrational faith, the sentence *"Credo quia
absurdum est"*[65]—"I believe *because* it is absurd"
—has full psychological validity. If somebody
makes a statement which is rationally sound, he
does what, in principle, everyone else can do.
If, however, he dares to make a statement which
is rationally absurd, he shows by this very fact
that he has transcended the faculty of common
sense and thus has a magic power which puts him
above the average person.

Among the abundance of historical examples of
irrational faith it would seem that the Biblical
report of the liberation of the Jews from the
Egyptian yoke is one of the most remarkable com-

[64] Adolf Hitler, *Mein Kampf* (New York: Reynal &
Hitchcock, Inc., 1939) ; p. 710.

[65] A popular, although somewhat distorted version of a
sentence by Tertullian.

ments on the problem of faith. In the whole report, the Jews are described as people who, though suffering from their enslavement, are afraid to rebel and unwilling to lose the security they have as slaves. They understand only the language of power, which they are afraid of but submit to; Moses, objecting to God's command that he announce himself as God's representative, says that the Jews will not believe in a god whose name they do not even know. God, although not wanting to assume a name, does so in order to satisfy the Jews' quest for certainty. Moses insists that even a name is not sufficient surety to make the Jews have faith in God. So God makes a further concession. He teaches Moses to perform miracles "in order that they may have faith that God appeared to you, the God of their fathers, the God of Abraham, Isaac and Jacob." The profound irony of this sentence is unmistakable. If the Jews had the kind of faith which God wished them to have, it would have been rooted in their own experience or the history of their nation; but they had become slaves, their faith was that of slaves and rooted in submission to power which proves its strength by its magic; they could be impressed only by another magic, not different from but only stronger than the one the Egyptians used.

The most drastic contemporary phenomenon of irrational faith is the faith in dictatorial leaders. Its defenders attempt to prove the genuineness of this faith by pointing to the fact that millions are ready to die for it. If faith is to be defined in terms of blind allegiance to a person or cause and measured by the readiness to give one's life for it, then indeed the faith of the Prophets in justice and love, and their opponents' faith in power is basically the same phenomenon, different only in its *object*. Then the faith of the defenders of freedom and that of their oppressors is only different inasmuch as it is a faith in different ideas.

Irrational faith is a fanatic conviction in somebody or something, rooted in submission to a personal or impersonal irrational authority. Rational faith, in contrast, is a firm conviction based on productive intellectual and emotional activity. In rational thinking, in which faith is supposed to have no place, rational faith is an important component. How does the scientist, for instance, arrive at a new discovery? Does he start with making experiment after experiment, gathering fact after fact without having a vision of what he expects to find? Rarely has any important discovery in any field been made in this way. Nor have people arrived at important conclusions when they were merely chasing a fantasy. The process of creative thinking in any field of human endeavor often starts with what may be called a "rational vision," itself a result of considerable previous study, reflective thinking, and observation. When the scientist succeeds in gathering enough data or in working out a mathematical formulation, or both, to make his original vision highly plausible he may be said to have arrived at a tentative hypothesis. A careful analysis of the hypothesis in order to discern its implications and the amassing of data which support it, lead to a more adequate hypothesis and eventually perhaps to its inclusion in a wide-ranging theory.

The history of science is replete with instances of faith in reason and vision of truth. Copernicus, Kepler, Galileo, and Newton were all imbued with an unshakable faith in reason. For this Bruno was burned at the stake and Spinoza suffered excommunication. At every step from the conception of a rational vision to the formulation of a theory, *faith* is necessary: faith in the vision as a rationally valid aim to pursue, faith in the hypothesis as a likely and plausible proposition, and faith in the final theory, at least until a general consensus about its validity has been reached.

This faith is rooted in one's own experience, in the confidence in one's power of thought, observation, and judgment. While irrational faith is the acceptance of something as true only *because* an authority or the majority say so, rational faith is rooted in an independent conviction based upon one's own productive observing and thinking.

Thought and judgment are not the only realm of experience in which rational faith is manifested. In the sphere of human relations, faith is an indispensable quality of any significant friendship or love. "Having faith" in another person means to be certain of the reliability and unchangeability of his fundamental attitudes, of the core of his personality. By this I do not mean that a person may not change his opinions but that his basic motivations remain the same; that, for instance, his capacity or respect for human dignity is part of his self, not subject to change.

In the same sense we have faith in ourselves. We are aware of the existence of a self, of a core in our personality which is unchangeable and which persists throughout our life in spite of varying circumstances and regardless of certain changes in opinions and feelings. It is this core which is the reality behind the word "I" and on which our conviction of our own identity is based. Unless we have faith in the persistence of our self, our feeling of identity is threatened and we become dependent on other people whose approval then becomes the basis for our feeling of identity with ourselves. Only the person who has faith in himself is able to be faithful to others because only he can be sure that he will be the same at a future time as he is today and, therefore, to feel and to act as he now expects to. Faith in oneself is a condition of our ability to promise something, and since, as Nietzsche pointed out, man can be defined by his capacity to promise, that is one of the conditions of human existence.

Another meaning of having faith in a person refers to the faith we have in the potentialities of others, of ourselves, and of mankind. The most rudimentary form in which this faith exists is the faith which the mother has toward her newborn baby: that it will live, grow, walk, and talk. However, the development of the child in this respect occurs with such regularity that the expectation of it does not seem to require faith. It is different with those potentialities which can fail to develop: the child's potentialities to love, to be happy, to use his reason, and more specific potentialities like artistic gifts. They are the seeds which grow and become manifest if the proper conditions for their development are given, and they can be stifled if they are absent. One of the most important of these conditions is that the significant persons in a child's life have faith in these potentialities. The presence of this faith makes the difference between education and manipulation. Education is identical with helping the child realize his potentialities.[66] The opposite of education is manipulation, which is based on the absence of faith in the growth of potentialities and on the conviction that a child will be right only if the adults put into him what is desirable and cut off what seems to be undesirable. There is no need of faith in the robot since there is no life in it either.

The faith in others has its culmination in faith in *mankind*. In the Western world this faith was expressed in religious terms in the Judaeo-Christian religion, and in secular language it has found its strongest expression in the progressive political and social ideas of the last 150 years. Like the faith in the child, it is based on the idea

---

[66] The root of the word education is *e-ducere*, literally, to lead forth, or to bring out something which is potentially present. Education in this sense results in *existence*, which means literally to stand out, to have emerged from the state of potentiality into that of manifest reality.

that the potentialities of man are such that given
the proper conditions they will be capable of building a social order governed by the principles of
equality, justice, and love. Man has not yet
achieved the building of such an order, and therefore the conviction that he can requires faith.
But like all rational faith this, too, is not wishful
thinking but based upon the evidence of the past
achievements of the human race and on the inner
experience of each individual, on his own experience of reason and love.

While irrational faith is rooted in the submission to a power which is felt to be overwhelmingly
strong, omniscient, and omnipotent, in the abdication of one's own power and strength, rational
faith is based upon the opposite experience. We
have this faith in a thought because it is a result
of our own observation and thinking. We have
faith in the potentialities of others, of ourselves,
and of mankind because, and only to the degree
to which, we have experienced the growth of our
own potentialities, the reality of growth in ourselves, the strength of our own power of reason
and of love. *The basis of rational faith is productiveness;* to live by our faith means to live productively and to have the only certainty which
exists: the certainty growing from productive
activity and from the experience that each one of
us is the active subject of whom these activities
are predicated. It follows that the belief in power
(in the sense of domination) and the use of power
are the reverse of faith. To believe in power that
exists is identical with disbelief in the growth of
potentialities which are as yet unrealized. It is a
prediction of the future based solely on the manifest present; but it turns out to be a grave mis-
calculation, profoundly irrational in its oversight
of human potentialities and human growth. There
is no rational faith in power. There is submission
to it or, on the part of those who have it, the wish

to keep it. While to many power seems to be the most real of all things, the history of man has proved it to be the most unstable of all human achievements. Because of the fact that faith and power are mutually exclusive, all religions and political systems which originally are built on rational faith become corrupt and eventually lose what strength they have if they rely on power or even ally themselves with it.

One misconception concerning faith must be briefly mentioned here. It is often assumed that faith is a state in which one passively waits for the realization of one's hope. While this is characteristic of irrational faith, it follows from our discussion that it is never true for rational faith. Inasmuch as rational faith is rooted in the experience of one's own productiveness, it cannot be passive but must be the expression of genuine inner activity. An old Jewish legend expresses this thought vividly. When Moses threw the wand into the Red Sea, the sea, quite contrary to the expected miracle, did not divide itself to leave a dry passage for the Jews. Not until the first man had jumped into the sea did the promised miracle happen and the waves recede.

At the outset of this discussion I differentiated between faith as an attitude, as a character trait, and faith as the belief in certain ideas or people. So far we have only dealt with faith in the former sense, and the question poses itself now whether there is any connection between faith as a character trait and the objects in which one has faith. It follows from our analysis of rational as against irrational faith that such a connection exists. Since rational faith is based upon our own productive experience, nothing can be its object which *transcends* human experience. Furthermore it follows that we cannot speak of rational faith when a person believes in the ideas of love, reason, and justice not as a result of his own experience but only because he has been taught such belief. Religious faith can be of either kind. Mainly some sects that did not share in the power of the church and some mystical currents in religion that emphasized man's own power to love, his likeness to God, have preserved and cultivated the attitude of rational faith in religious symbolism. What holds true of religions holds true for faith in its secular form, particularly in political and social ideas. The ideas of freedom or democracy deteriorate into nothing but irrational faith once they are not based upon the productive experience of each individual but are presented to him by parties or states which force him to believe in these ideas. There is much less difference between a mystic faith in God and an atheist's rational faith in mankind than between the former's faith and that of a Calvinist whose faith in God is rooted in the conviction of his own powerlessness and in his fear of God's power.

Man cannot live without faith. The crucial question for our own generation and the next ones is whether this faith will be an irrational faith in leaders, machines, success, or the rational faith in man based on the experience of our own productive activity.

5. *The Moral Powers in Man*

Wonders are many, and none is more wonderful than man.

—Sophocles, *Antigone*

A. MAN, GOOD OR EVIL?

The position taken by humanistic ethics that man is able to know what is good and to act accordingly on the strength of his natural potentialities and of his reason would be untenable if the dogma of man's innate natural evilness were

true. The opponents of humanistic ethics claim
that man's nature is such as to make him inclined
to be hostile to his fellow men, to be envious and
jealous, and to be lazy, unless he is curbed by fear.
Many representatives of humanistic ethics met
this challenge by insisting that man is inherently
good and that destructiveness is not an integral
part of his nature.

Indeed, the controversy between these two conflicting views is one of the basic themes in Western thought. To Socrates, ignorance, and not
man's natural disposition, was the source of evilness; to him vice was error. The Old Testament,
on the contrary, tells us that man's history starts
with an act of sin, and that his "strivings are evil
from childhood on." In the early Middle Ages the
battle between the two opposing views was centered around the question of how to interpret the
Biblical myth of Adam's fall. Augustine thought
that man's nature was corrupt since the fall, that
each generation was born with the curse caused by
the first man's disobedience, and that only God's
grace, transmitted by the Church and her sacra-
ments, could save man. Pelagius, Augustine's
great adversary, held that Adam's sin was purely
personal and had affected none but himself; that
every man, consequently, is born with powers as
incorrupt as Adam's before the fall, and that sin
is the result of temptation and evil example. The
battle was won by Augustine, and this victory
was to determine—and to darken—man's mind
for centuries.

The late Middle Ages witnessed an increasing
belief in man's dignity, power, and natural goodness. The thinkers of the Renaissance as well as
theologians like Thomas Aquinas of the thirteenth
century gave expression to this belief, although
their views on man differed in many essential
points and although Aquinas never reverted to
the radicalism of the Pelagian "heresy." The

antithesis, the idea of man's intrinsic evilness, was expressed in Luther's and Calvin's doctrines, thus reviving the Augustinian position. While insisting on man's spiritual freedom and on his right—and obligation—to face God directly and without the priest as an intermediary, they denounced man's intrinsic evilness and powerlessness. According to them the greatest obstacle to man's salvation is his pride; and he can overcome it only by guilt feelings, repentance, unqualified submission to God, and faith in God's mercy.

These two threads remain interwoven in the texture of modern thought. The idea of man's dignity and power was pronounced by the enlightenment philosophy, by progressive, liberal thought of the nineteenth century, and most radically by Nietzsche. The idea of man's worthlessness and nothingness found a new, and this time entirely secularized, expression in the authoritarian systems in which the state or "society" became the supreme rulers, while the individual, recognizing his own insignificance, is supposed to find his fulfillment in obedience and submission. The two ideas, while clearly separated in the philosophies of democracy and authoritarianism, are blended in their less extreme forms in the thinking, and still more so in the feeling, of our culture. Today, we are adherents both of Augustine *and* Pelagius, of Luther *and* Pico della Mirandola, of Hobbes *and* Jefferson. We consciously believe in man's power and dignity, but—often unconsciously—we also believe in man's—and particularly our own—powerlessness and badness and explain it by pointing to "human nature."[67]

In Freud's writings the two opposing ideas have found expression in terms of psychological theory.

[67] R. Niebuhr, the exponent of contemporary neo-orthodox theology, has made the Lutheran position explicit again, combining it, paradoxically, with a progressive political philosophy.

Freud was in many respects a typical representative of the Enlightenment spirit, believing in reason and in man's right to protect his natural claims against social conventions and cultural pressure. At the same time, however, he held the view that man was lazy and self-indulgent by nature and had to be forced into the path of socially useful activity.[68] The most radical expression of the view of man's innate destructiveness is to be found in Freud's theory of the "death-instinct." After the first World War he was so impressed by the power of destructive passion that he revised his older theory, according to which there were two types of instincts, sex and self-preservation, by giving a dominant place to irrational destructiveness. He assumed that man was the battlefield on which two equally powerful forces meet: the drive to live and the drive to die. These, he thought, were biological forces to be found in all organisms, including man. If the drive to die was turned to outside objects, it manifested itself as a drive to destroy; if it remained within the organism, it aimed at self-destruction.

Freud's theory is dualistic. He does not see man as either essentially good or essentially evil, but as being driven by two equally strong contradictory forces. The same dualistic view had been expressed in many religious and philosophical systems. Life and death, love and strife, day and night, white and black, Ormuzd and Ahriman are only some of the many symbolic formulations of this polarity. Such dualistic theory is indeed very appealing to the student of human nature. It leaves room for the idea of the goodness of man, but it also accounts for man's tremendous capacity for destructiveness which only superficial, wishful thinking can ignore. The dualistic position, how-

---

[68] The two opposing sides of Freud's attitude are to be found in his *The Future of an Illusion.*

ever, is only the starting point and not the answer to our psychological and ethical problem. Are we to understand this dualism to mean that both the drive to live and the drive to destroy are innate and equally strong capacities in man? In this case humanistic ethics would be confronted with the problem of how the destructive side in man's nature can be curbed without sanctions and authoritarian commands.

Or can we arrive at an answer more congenial to the principle of humanistic ethics and can the polarity between the striving for life and the striving for destruction be understood in a different sense? Our ability to answer these questions depends on the insight we have into the nature of hostility and destructiveness. But before entering into this discussion we would do well to be aware of how much depends on the answer for the problem of ethics.

The choice between life and death is indeed the basic alternative of ethics. It is the alternative between productiveness and destructiveness, between potency and impotence, between virtue and vice. For humanistic ethics all evil strivings are directed against life and all good serves the preservation and unfolding of life.

Our first step in approaching the problem of destructiveness is to differentiate between two kinds of hate: rational, "reactive" and irrational, "character-conditioned" hate. *Reactive, rational* hate is a person's reaction to a threat to his own or another person's freedom, life, or ideas. Its premise is respect for life. Rational hate has an important biological function: it is the affective equivalent of action serving the protection of life; it comes into existence as a reaction to vital threats, and it ceases to exist when the threat has been removed; *it is not the opposite but the concomitant of the striving for life.*

Character-conditioned hate is different in qual-

ity. It is a character trait, a continuous readiness
to hate, lingering within the person who *is* hostile
rather than reacting with hate to a stimulus from
without. Irrational hate can be actualized by the
same kind of realistic threat which arouses reactive hate; but often it is a gratuitous hate, using
every opportunity to be expressed, rationalized
as reactive hate. The hating person seems to have
a feeling of relief, as though he were happy to
have found the opportunity to express his lingering hostility. One can almost see in his face the
pleasure he derives from the satisfaction of his
hatred.

Ethics is concerned primarily with the problem
of irrational hate, the passion to destroy or cripple
life. Irrational hate is rooted in a person's character, its object being of secondary importance.
It is directed against others as well as against
oneself, although we are more often aware of hating others than of hating ourselves. The hate
against ourselves is usually rationalized as sacrifice, selflessness, asceticism, or as self-accusation
and inferiority feeling.

The frequency of *reactive* hate is even greater
than it may appear, because often a person reacts
with hate toward threats against his integrity
and freedom, threats which are not obvious and
explicit but subtle or even disguised as love and
protection. But even so, character hate remains a
phenomenon of such magnitude that the dualistic
theory of love and hate as the two fundamental
forces seems to fit the facts. I have to concede,
then, the correctness of the dualistic theory? In
order to answer this question we need to inquire
further into the nature of this dualism. Are the
good and evil forces of equal strength? Are they
both part of the original equipment of man, or
what other possible relation could exist between
them?

According to Freud destructiveness is inherent

in all human beings; it differs mainly with regard to the object of destructiveness—others or themselves. From this position it would follow that destructiveness against oneself is in reverse proportion to that against others. This assumption, however, is contradicted by the fact that people differ in the degree of their total destructiveness, regardless of whether it is primarily directed against themselves or against others. We do not find great destructiveness against others in those who have little hostility against themselves; on the contrary we see that hostility against oneself and others is conjunctive. We find furthermore that the life-destructive forces in a person occur in an inverse ratio to the life-furthering ones; the stronger the one, the weaker the other, and vice versa. This fact offers a clue to the understanding of the life-destructive energy; it would seem that the degree of destructiveness is proportionate to the degree to which the unfolding of a person's capacities is blocked. I am not referring here to occasional frustrations of this or that desire but to the blockage of spontaneous expression of man's sensory, emotional, physical, and intellectual capacities, to the thwarting of his productive potentialities. If life's tendency to grow, to be lived, is thwarted, the energy thus blocked undergoes a process of *change* and is transformed into life-destructive energy. *Destructiveness is the outcome of unlived life.* Those individual and social conditions which make for the blocking of life-furthering energy produce destructiveness which in turn is the source from which the various manifestations of evil spring.

If it is true that destructiveness must develop as a result of blocked productive energy it would seem that it can rightly be called a potentiality in man's nature. Does it follow then that both good and evil are potentialities of equal strength in man? In order to answer this question we must inquire into the meaning of potentiality. To say that something exists "potentially" means not only that it will exist in the future but that this future existence is already prepared in the present. This relationship between the present and the future stage of development can be described by saying that the future virtually exists in the present. Does this mean that the future stage will *necessarily* come into being if the present stage exists? Obviously not. If we say that the tree is potentially present in the seed it does not mean that a tree *must* develop from every seed. The actualization of a potentiality depends on the presence of certain conditions which are, in the case of the seed, for instance, proper soil, water, and sunlight. In fact, the concept of potentiality has no meaning except in connection with the specific conditions required for its actualization. The statement that the tree is potentially present in the seed must be specified to mean that a tree will grow from the seed *provided* that the seed is placed in the specific conditions necessary for its growth. If these proper conditions are absent, if, for instance, the soil is too moist and thus incompatible with the seed's growth, the latter will not develop into a tree but rot. If an animal is deprived of food, it will not realize its potentiality for growth but will die. It may be said, then, that the seed or the animal has two kinds of potentialities, from each of which certain results follow in a later stage of development: one, a *primary potentiality* which is actualized if the proper conditions are present; the other, a *secondary potentiality*, which is actualized if conditions are in contrast to existential needs. Both the primary and the secondary potentialities are part of the nature of an organism. The secondary potentialities become manifest with the same necessity as does the primary potentiality. The terms "primary" and "secondary" are used in order to de-

note that the development of the potentiality
called "primary" occurs under normal conditions
and that the "secondary" potentiality comes into
manifest existence only in case of abnormal, pathogenic conditions.

Provided we are right in assuming that destructiveness is a secondary potentiality in man
which becomes manifest only if he fails to realize
his primary potentialities, we have answered only
one of the objections to humanistic ethics. We
have shown that man is not necessarily evil but
becomes evil only if the proper conditions for his
growth and development are lacking. The evil has
no independent existence of its own, it is the
absence of the good, the result of the failure to
realize life.

We have to deal with still another objection to
humanistic ethics which says that the proper conditions for the development of the good must
comprise rewards and punishment because man
has not within himself any incentive for the development of his powers. I shall attempt to show in
the following pages that the normal individual
possesses in himself the tendency to develop, to
grow, and to be productive, and that the paralysis
of this tendency is in itself the symptom of mental
sickness. Mental health, like physical health, is
not an aim to which the individual must be forced
from the outside but one the incentive for which
is in the individual and the suppression of which
requires strong environmental forces operating
against him.[69]

The assumption that man has an inherent drive
for growth and integration does not imply an
abstract drive for perfection as a particular gift
with which man is endowed. It follows from the
very nature of man, from the principle that *the
power to act creates a need to use this power and*

[69] This view has been strongly emphasized by K. Gold-
stein, H. S. Sullivan and K. Horney.

that the failure to use it results in dysfunction and unhappiness. The validity of this principle can be easily recognized with regard to the physiological functions of man. Man has the power to walk and to move; if he were prevented from using this power severe physical discomfort or illness would result. Women have the power to bear children and to nurse them; if this power remains unused, if a woman does not become a mother, if she can not spend her power to bear and love a child, she experiences a frustration which can be remedied only by increased realization of her powers in other realms of her life. Freud has called attention to another lack of expenditure as a cause of suffering, that of sexual energy, by recognizing that the blocking of sexual energy can be the cause of neurotic disturbances. While Freud overvalued the significance of sexual satisfaction, his theory is a profound *symbolic* expression of the fact that man's failure to use and to spend what he has is the cause of sickness and unhappiness. The validity of this principle is apparent with regard to psychic as well as physical powers. Man is endowed with the capacities of speaking and thinking. If these powers were blocked, the person would be severely damaged. Man has the power to love, and if he can not make use of his power, if he is incapable of loving, he suffers from this misfortune even though he may try to ignore his suffering by all kinds of rationalizations or by using the culturally patterned avenues of escape from the pain caused by his failure.

The reason for the phenomenon that not using one's powers results in unhappiness is to be found in the very condition of human existence. Man's existence is characterized by existential dichotomies which I have discussed in a previous chapter. He has no other way to be one with the world and at the same time to feel one with himself, to be related to others and to retain his integrity as a unique entity, but by making productive use of his powers. If he fails to do so, he can not achieve inner harmony and integration; he is torn and split, driven to escape from himself, from the feeling of powerlessness, boredom and impotence which are the necessary results of his failure. Man, being alive, can not help wishing to live and the only way he can succeed in the act of living is to use his powers, to spend that which he has.

There is perhaps no phenomenon which shows more clearly the result of man's failure in productive and integrated living than neurosis. Every neurosis is the result of a conflict between man's inherent powers and those forces which block their development. Neurotic symptoms, like the symptoms of a physical sickness, are the expression of the fight which the healthy part of the personality puts up against the crippling influences directed against its unfolding.

However, lack of integration and productiveness does not *always* lead to neurosis. As a matter of fact, if this were the case, we would have to consider the vast majority of people as neurotic. What, then, are the specific conditions which make for the neurotic outcome? There are some conditions which I can mention only briefly: for example, one child may be broken more thoroughly than others, and the conflict between his anxiety and his basic human desires may, therefore, be sharper and more unbearable; or the child may have developed a sense of freedom and originality which is greater than that of the average person, and the defeat may thus be more unacceptable.

But instead of enumerating other conditions which make for neurosis, I prefer to reverse the question and ask what the conditions are which are responsible for the fact that so many people do *not* become neurotic in spite of the failure in productive and integrated living. It seems to be useful at this point to differentiate between two concepts: that of defect, and that of neurosis.[70] If a person fails to attain maturity, spontaneity, and a genuine experience of self, he may be considered to have a severe defect, provided we assume that freedom and spontaneity are the objective goals to be attained by every human being. If such a goal is not attained by the majority of members of any given society, we deal with the phenomenon of *socially patterned defect*. The individual shares it with many others; he is not aware of it as a defect, and his security is not threatened by the experience of being different, of being an outcast, as it were. What he may have lost in richness and in a genuine feeling of happiness is made up by the security he feels of fitting in with the rest of mankind—*as he knows them.* As a matter of fact, his very defect may have been raised to a virtue by his culture and thus give him an enhanced feeling of achievement. An illustration is the feeling of guilt and anxiety which Calvin's doctrines aroused in men. It may be said that the person who is overwhelmed by a feeling of his own powerlessness and unworthiness, by the unceasing doubt of whether he is saved or condemned to eternal punishment, who is hardly capable of any genuine joy and has made himself into the cog of a machine which he has to serve, that such a person, indeed, has a severe defect. Yet this very defect was culturally patterned; it was looked upon as particularly valuable, and the individual was thus protected from the neurosis which he would have acquired in a culture where the defect would give him a feeling of profound inadequacy and isolation.

Spinoza has formulated the problem of the

[70] The following discussion of neurosis and defect is partly taken from my paper, "Individual and Social Origins of Neurosis," *American Sociological Review*, IX, No. 4 (August, 1944).

socially patterned defect very clearly. He says:
"Many people are seized by one and the same
affect with great consistency. All his senses are
so strongly affected by one object that he believes
this object to be present even if it is not. If this
happens while the person is awake, the person is
believed to be insane. . . . But if the *greedy* person thinks only of money and possessions, the
ambitious one only of fame, one does not think of
them as being insane, but only as annoying;
generally one has contempt for them. But *factually*
greediness, ambition, and so forth are forms of
insanity, although usually one does not think
of them as 'illness.' "[71] These words were written
a few hundred years ago; they still hold true,
although the defect has been culturally patterned
to such an extent now that it is not generally
thought any more to be contemptible or even
annoying. Today we can meet a person who acts
and feels like an automaton; we find that he never
experiences anything which is really his; that he
experiences himself entirely as the person he
thinks he is supposed to be; that smiles have replaced laughter, meaningless chatter replaced
communicative speech and dulled despair has
taken the place of genuine sadness. Two statements can be made about this kind of person. One
is that he suffers from a defect of spontaneity and
individuality which may seem incurable. At the
same time it may be said that he does not differ
essentially from thousands of others who are in
the same position. With *most* of them the cultural
pattern provided for the defect saves them from
the outbreak of neurosis. With *some* the cultural
pattern does not function, and the defect appears
as a more or less severe neurosis. The fact that
in these cases the cultural pattern does not suffice
to prevent the outbreak of a manifest neurosis is

[71] *Ethic*, IV, Prop. 44, Schol.

a result either of the greater intensity of the pathological forces or of the greater strength of the healthy forces which put up a fight even though the cultural pattern would permit them to remain silent.

There is no situation which provides for a better opportunity to observe the strength and tenacity of the forces striving for health than that of psychoanalytic therapy. To be sure, the psychoanalyst is confronted with the strength of those forces which operate against a person's self-realization and happiness, but when he can understand the power of those conditions—particularly in childhood—which made for the crippling of productiveness he cannot fail to be impressed by the fact that most of his patients would long since have given up the fight were they not impelled by an impulse to achieve psychic health and happiness. This very impulse is the necessary condition for the cure of neurosis. While the process of psychoanalysis consists in gaining greater insight into the dissociated parts of a person's feelings and ideas, intellectual insight as such is not a sufficient condition for change. This kind of insight enables a person to recognize the blind alleys in which he is caught and to understand why his attempts to solve his problem were doomed to failure; but it only clears the way for those forces in him which strive for psychic health and happiness to operate and to become effective. Indeed, merely intellectual insight is not sufficient; the therapeutically effective insight is experiential insight in which knowledge of oneself has not only an intellectual but also an affective quality. Such experiential insight itself depends on the strength of man's inherent striving for health and happiness.

The problem of psychic health and neurosis is inseparably linked up with that of ethics. It may be said that every neurosis represents a moral problem. The failure to achieve maturity and integration of the whole personality is a moral failure in the sense of humanistic ethics. In a more specific sense many neuroses are the expression of moral problems, and neurotic symptoms result from unsolved moral conflicts. A man, for instance, may suffer from spells of dizziness for which there is no organic cause. In reporting his symptom to the psychoanalyst he mentions casually that he is coping with certain difficulties in his job. He is a successful teacher who has to express views which run counter to his own convictions. He believes, however, that he has solved the problem of being successful, on the one hand, and of having preserved his moral integrity, on the other, and he "proves" to himself the correctness of this belief by a number of complicated rationalizations. He is annoyed at the suggestion of the analyst that his symptom may have something to do with his moral problem. However, the ensuing analysis shows that he was wrong in his belief, his spells of dizziness were the reaction of his better self, of his basically moral personality to a pattern of life which forced him to violate his integrity and to cripple his spontaneity.

Even if a person seems to be destructive only of others, he violates the principle of life in himself as well as in others. In religious language this principle has been expressed in terms of man's being created in the image of God, and thus any violation of man is a sin against God. In secular language we would say that everything we do— good or evil—to another human being we also do to ourselves. *"Do not do to others what you would not have them do to you"* is one of the most fundamental principles of ethics. But it is equally justifiable to state: *Whatever you do to others, you also do to yourself.* To violate the forces directed toward life in any human being necessarily has repercussions on ourselves. Our own growth, happiness, and strength are based on the respect for these forces, and one cannot violate them in others and remain untouched oneself at the same time. The respect for life, that of others as well as one's own, is the concomitant of the process of life itself and a condition of psychic health. In a way, destructiveness against others is a pathological phenomenon comparable to suicidal impulses. While a person may succeed in ignoring or rationalizing destructive impulses, he—his organism as it were—cannot help reacting and being affected by acts which contradict the very principle by which his life and all life are sustained. We find that the destructive person is unhappy even if he has succeeded in attaining the aims of his destructiveness, which undermines his own existence. Conversely, no healthy person can help admiring, and being affected by, manifestations of decency, love, and courage; for these are the forces on which his own life rests.

B. REPRESSION VS. PRODUCTIVENESS

The position that man is basically destructive and selfish leads to a concept which maintains that ethical behavior consists in the suppression of these evil strivings in which man would indulge without exercising constant self-control. Man, according to this principle, must be his own watchdog; he must, in the first place, recognize that his nature is evil, and, in the second, use his will power to fight his inherent evil tendencies. Suppression of evil or indulgence in it would then be his alternative.

Psychoanalytic research offers a wealth of data concerning the nature of suppression, its various kinds, and their consequences. We can differentiate between (1) suppression of the *acting out* of an evil impulse, (2) suppression of the *awareness* of the impulse, and (3) a constructive fight against the impulse.

In the first kind of suppression not the impulse itself is suppressed but the action which would follow from it. A case in point is a person with strong sadistic strivings who would be satisfied and pleased to make others suffer or to dominate them. Suppose his fear of disapproval or the moral precepts he has accepted tell him that he should not act upon his impulse; hence he refrains from such action and does not do what he would wish to do. While one can not deny that this person has achieved a victory over himself, he has not really changed; his character has remained the same and what we can admire in him is only his "will power." But quite aside from the moral evaluation of such behavior, it is unsatisfactory in its effectiveness as a safeguard against man's destructive tendencies. It would require an extraordinary amount of "will power" or of fear of severe sanctions to keep such a person from acting according to his impulse. Since every decision would be the result of an inner battle against strong opposing forces, the chances for the triumph of the good would be so precarious that from the standpoint of the interest of society this type of suppression is too unreliable.

By far the more effective way to deal with evil strivings would seem to be to hinder them from becoming conscious, so that there is no conscious temptation. This kind of suppression is what Freud called "repression." Repression means that the impulse, although it exists, is not permitted to enter the realm of consciousness or is quickly removed from it. To use the same illustration, the sadistic person would not be aware of his wish to destroy or to dominate; there would be no temptation and no struggle.

Repression of evil strivings is that kind of suppression upon which authoritarian ethics relies implicitly or explicitly as the safest road to virtue. But while it is true that repression is a safeguard against action, it is much less effective than its advocates believe it to be.

Repressing an impulse means removing it from awareness but it does not mean removing it from existence. Freud has shown that the repressed impulse continues to operate and to exercise a profound influence upon the person although the person is not aware of it. The effect of the repressed impulse on the person is not even necessarily smaller than if it were conscious; the main difference is that it is not acted upon overtly but in disguise, so that the person acting is spared the knowledge of what he is doing. Our sadistic person, for instance, not being aware of his sadism, may have the feeling that he dominates other people out of concern for what—he thinks—would be best for them or because of his strong sense of duty.

But as Freud has shown, the repressed strivings are not acted out in such rationalizations only. A person, for instance, may develop a "reaction-formation," the very opposite of the repressed striving, as, for instance, oversolicitousness or overkindness. Yet the power of the repressed striving becomes apparent indirectly, a phenomenon which Freud called "the return of the repressed." In this case a person whose oversolicitousness has developed as a reaction-formation against his sadism may use this "virtue" with the same effect his manifest sadism would have had: to dominate and to control. While *he* feels virtuous and superior, the effect on others is often even more devastating because it is hard to defend oneself against too much "virtue."

Entirely different from suppression and repression is a third type of reaction to destructive impulses. While in suppression the impulse remains alive and only the action is prohibited, and

while in repression the impulse itself is removed
from consciousness and is acted upon (to some
extent) in disguised fashion, in this third type of
reaction the life-furthering forces in a person
fight against the destructive and evil impulses.
The more aware a person is of the latter the more
is he able to react. Not only his will and his
reason take part, but those emotional forces in
him which are challenged by his destructiveness.
In a sadistic person, for instance, such a fight
against sadism will develop a genuine kindness
which becomes part of his character and relieves
him from the task of being his own watchdog and
of using his will power constantly for "self-
control." In this reaction the emphasis is not on
one's feeling of badness and remorse but on the
presence and use of productive forces within man.
Thus, as a result of the productive conflict between
good and evil, the evil itself becomes a source of
virtue.

It follows from the standpoint of humanistic
ethics that the ethical alternative is not between
suppression of evil or indulgence in it. Both—
repression and indulgence—are only two aspects
of bondage, and the real ethical alternative is
not between them but between repression-indul-
gence on the one hand and productiveness on the
other. The aim of humanistic ethics is not the
repression of man's evilness (which is fostered
by the crippling effect of the authoritarian spirit)
but the productive use of man's inherent primary
potentialities. Virtue is proportional to the degree
of productiveness a person has achieved. If society
is concerned with making people virtuous, it must
be concerned with making them productive and
hence with creating the conditions for the development of productiveness. The first and foremost
of these conditions is that the unfolding and
growth of every person is the aim of all social and
political activities, that man is the only purpose

and end, and not a means for anybody or anything except himself.

The productive orientation is the basis for freedom, virtue, and happiness. Vigilance is the price of virtue, but not the vigilance of the guard who has to shut in the evil prisoner; rather, the vigilance of the rational being who has to recognize and to create the conditions for his productiveness and to do away with those factors which block him and thus create the evil which, once it has arisen, can be prevented from becoming manifest only by external or internal force.

Authoritarian ethics has imbued people with the idea that to be good would require a tremendous and relentless effort; that man has to fight himself constantly and that every false step he makes could be disastrous. This view follows from the authoritarian premise. If man were such an evil being and if virtue were only the victory over himself, then indeed the task would seem appallingly difficult. But if virtue is the same as productiveness, its achievement is, though not simple, by no means such a laborious and difficult enterprise. As we have shown, the wish to make productive use of his powers is inherent in man, and his efforts consist mainly in removing the obstacles in himself and in his environment which block him from following his inclination. Just as the person who has become sterile and destructive is increasingly paralyzed and caught, as it were, in a *vicious circle*, a person who is aware of his own powers and uses them productively gains in strength, faith, and happiness, and is less and less in danger of being alienated from himself; he has created, as we might say, a "virtuous circle." The experience of joy and happiness is not only, as we have shown, the *result* of productive living but also its *stimulus*. Repression of evilness may spring from a spirit of self-castigation and sorrow, but there is nothing more conducive to goodness in the humanistic sense than the experience of joy and happiness which accompanies any productive activity. Every increase in joy a culture can provide for will do more for the ethical education of its members than all the warnings of punishment or preachings of virtue could do.

C. CHARACTER AND MORAL JUDGMENT

The problem of moral judgment is frequently associated with that of freedom of will vs. determinism. One view holds that man is completely determined by circumstances which he can not control, and that the idea that man is free in his decisions is nothing but an illusion. From this premise the conclusion is drawn that man can not be judged for his actions since he is not free in making his decisions. The opposite view maintains that man has the faculty of free will, which he can exercise regardless of psychological or external conditions and circumstances; hence that he is responsible for his actions and can be judged by them.

It would seem that the psychologist is compelled to subscribe to determinism. In studying the development of character he recognizes that the child starts his life in an indifferent moral state, and that his character is shaped by external influences which are most powerful in the early years of his life, when he has neither the knowledge nor the power to change the circumstances which determine his character. At an age when he might attempt to change the conditions under which he lives, his character is already formed and he lacks the incentive to investigate these conditions and to change them, if necessary. If we assume that the moral qualities of a person are rooted in his character, is it not true, then, that since he has no freedom in shaping his character, he cannot be judged? Is it not true that the more insight we have into the conditions which are responsible for the formation of character and its dynamics, the more inescapable seems the view that no person can be morally judged?

Perhaps we can avoid this alternative between psychological understanding and moral judgment by a compromise which is sometimes suggested by the adherents of the free will theory. It is maintained that there are circumstances in the lives of people which preclude the exercise of their free will and thus eliminate moral judgment. Modern criminal law, for instance, has accepted this view and does not hold an insane person responsible for his actions. The proponents of a modified theory of free will go one step further and admit that a person who is not insane but neurotic, and thus under the sway of impulses which he can not control, may also not be judged for his actions. They claim, however, that most people have the freedom to act well if they want to and that therefore they must be morally judged.

But closer examination shows that even this view is untenable. We are prone to believe that we act freely because, as Spinoza has already suggested, we are aware of our wishes but unaware of their motivations. Our motives are an outcome of the particular blend of forces operating in our character. Each time we make a decision it is determined by the good or evil forces, respectively, which are dominant. In some people one particular force is so overwhelmingly strong that the outcome of their decisions can be predicted by anyone who knows their character and the prevailing standards of values (although they themselves might be under the illusion of having decided "freely"). In others, destructive and constructive forces are balanced in such a way that their decisions are not empirically predictable. When we say a person could have acted differently we refer to the latter case. But to say he could have acted differently means only that we could not have predicted his actions. His decision, however, shows that one set of forces was stronger than the other and hence that even in his case his decision was determined by his character. Therefore, if his character had been different he would have acted differently, but again strictly according to the structure of his character. The will is not an abstract power of man which he possesses apart from his character. On the contrary, the will is nothing but the expression of his character. The productive person who trusts his reason and who is capable of loving others and himself has the will to act virtuously. The nonproductive person who has failed to develop these qualities and who is a slave of his irrational passions lacks this will.

The view that it is our character which determines our decisions is by no means fatalistic. Man, while like all other creatures subject to forces which determine him, is the only creature endowed with reason, the only being who is capable of understanding the very forces which he is subjected to and who by his understanding can take an active part in his own fate and strengthen those elements which strive for the good. Man is the only creature endowed with conscience. His conscience is the voice which calls him back to himself, it permits him to know what he ought to do in order to become himself, it helps him to remain aware of the aims of his life and of the norms necessary for the attainment of these aims. We are therefore not helpless victims of circumstance; we are, indeed, able to change and to influence forces inside and outside ourselves and to control, at least to some extent, the conditions which play upon us. We can foster and enhance those conditions which develop the striving for good and bring about its realization. But while we have reason and conscience, which enable us to be active participants in our life, reason and conscience themselves are inseparably linked up with our character. If destructive forces and irrational passions have gained dominance in our character, both our reason and our conscience are affected and cannot exercise their function properly. Indeed, the latter are our most precious capacities which it is our task to develop and to use; but they are not free and undetermined and they do not exist apart from our empirical self; they are forces within the structure of our total personality and, like every part of a structure, determined by the structure as a whole, and determining it.

If we base our moral judgment of a person on the decision as to whether or not he could have willed differently, no moral judgment can be made. How can we know, for instance, the strength of a person's innate vitality that made it possible for him to resist environmental forces acting upon him in his childhood and later on; or the lack of vitality that makes another person submit to the very same forces? How can we know whether in one person's life an accidental event such as the contact with a good and loving person might not have influenced his character development in one direction while the absence of such an experience might have influenced it in the opposite direction? Indeed, we can not know. Even if we would base moral judgment on the premise that a person could have acted differently, the constitutional and environmental factors which make for the development of his character are so numerous and complex that it is impossible, for all practical purposes, to arrive at a conclusive judgment whether or not he could have developed differently. All we can assume is that circumstances as they were led to the development as it occurred. It follows that if our ability to judge a person depended on our knowledge that he could have acted differently, we, as students of character, would have to admit defeat as far as ethical judgments are concerned.

Yet this conclusion is unwarranted because it is based on false premises and on confusion about the meaning of judgment. To judge can mean two different things: to judge means to exercise the mental functions of assertion or predication. But "to judge" means also to have the function of a "judge" referring to the activity of absolving and condemning.

The latter kind of moral judging is based upon the idea of an authority transcending man and passing judgment on him. This authority is privileged to absolve or to condemn and punish. Its dicta are absolute, because it is above man and empowered with wisdom and strength unattainable by him. Even the picture of the judge, who, in democratic society, is elected and theoretically not above his fellow men, is tinged by the old concept of a judging god. Although his person does not carry any superhuman power, his office does. (The forms of respect due the judge are surviving remnants of the respect due a superhuman authority; contempt of court is psychologically closely related to *lèse-majesté*.) But many persons who have not the office of a judge assume the role of a judge, ready to condemn or absolve, when they make moral judgments. Their attitude often contains a good deal of sadism and destructiveness. There is perhaps no phenomenon which contains so much destructive feeling as "moral indignation," which permits envy or hate to be acted out under the guise of virtue.[72] The "indignant" person has for once the satisfaction of despising and treating a creature as "inferior," coupled

---

[72] A. Ranulf's book, *Moral Indignation and the Middle Class*, is an excellent illustration of this point. The title of the book could just as well be "Sadism and the Middle Class."

with the feeling of his own superiority and right-
eousness.

Humanistic judgment of ethical values has the
same logical character as a rational judgment in
general. In making value judgments one judges
facts and does not feel one is godlike, superior,
and entitled to condemn or forgive. A judgment
that a person is destructive, greedy, jealous, envious is not different from a physician's statement
about a dysfunction of the heart or the lungs.
Suppose we have to judge a murderer whom we
know to be a pathological case. If we could learn
all about his heredity, his early and later environment, we would very likely come to the conclusion
that he was completely under the sway of conditions over which he had no power; in fact, much
more so than a petty thief and, therefore, much
more "understandable" than the latter. But this
does not mean that we ought not to judge his
evilness. We can understand *how* and *why* he
became what he is, but we can also judge him as
to *what* he is. We can even assume that we would
have become like him had we lived under the
same circumstances; but while such considerations prevent us from assuming a godlike role,
they do not prevent us from moral judgment. The
problem of understanding versus judging character is not different from the understanding and
judging of any other human performance. If I
have to judge the value of a pair of shoes or that
of a painting, I do so according to certain objective
standards intrinsic to the objects. Assuming the
shoes or the painting to be of poor quality, and
that somebody pointed to the fact that the shoemaker or the painter had tried very hard but that
certain conditions made it impossible for him to
do better, I will not in either case change my
judgment of the product. I may feel sympathy or
pity for the shoemaker or the painter, I may feel
tempted to help him, but I can not say that I can

not judge his work because I understand *why* it is so poor.

Man's main task in life is to give birth to himself, to become what he potentially is. The most important product of his effort is his own personality. One can judge objectively to what extent the person has succeeded in his task, to what degree he has realized his potentialities. If he failed in his task, one can recognize this failure and judge it for what it is—his moral failure. Even if one knows that the odds against the person were overwhelming and that everyone else would have failed too, the judgment about him remains the same. If one fully understands all the circumstances which made him as he is, one may have compassion for him; yet this compassion does not alter the validity of the judgment. Understanding a person does not mean condoning; it only means that one does not accuse him as if one were God or a judge placed above him.

6. Absolute vs. Relative, Universal vs. Socially Immanent Ethics

We see men sometimes so affected by one object, that although it is not present, they believe it to be before them; and if this happens to a man who is not asleep, we say that he is delirious or mad. Nor are those believed to be less mad who are inflamed by love, dreaming about nothing but a mistress or harlot day and night, for they excite our laughter. But the avaricious man who thinks of nothing else but gain or money, and the ambitious man who thinks of nothing but glory, inasmuch as they do harm, and are, therefore, thought worthy of hatred, are not believed to be mad. In truth, however, avarice, ambition, lust, etc., are a kind of madness, although they are not reckoned amongst diseases.

—Spinoza, *Ethics*

The discussion of absolute as against relative ethics has been considerably and unnecessarily confused by the uncritical use of the terms "absolute" and "relative." An attempt will be made in this chapter to differentiate their several connotations and to discuss the different meanings separately.

The first meaning in which "absolute" ethics is used holds that ethical propositions are unquestionably and eternally true and neither permit nor warrant revision. This concept of absolute ethics is to be found in authoritarian systems, and it follows logically from the premise that the criterion of validity is the unquestionable superior and omniscient power of the authority. It is the very essence of this claim to superiority that the authority can not err and that its commands and prohibitions are eternally true. We can be very brief in disposing of the idea that ethical norms in order to be valid have to be "absolute." This concept, which is based on the theistic premise of the existence of an "absolute" = perfect power in comparison with which man is necessarily "relative" = imperfect has been superseded in all other fields of scientific thought, where it is generally recognized that there is no absolute truth but nevertheless that there are objectively valid laws and principles. As has been previously pointed out, a scientific or a rationally valid statement means that the power of reason is applied to all the available data of observation without any of them being suppressed or falsified for the sake of a desired result. The history of science is a history of inadequate and incomplete statements, and every new insight makes possible the recognition of the inadequacies of previous propositions and offers a springboard for creating a more adequate formulation. The history of thought is the history of an ever-increasing approximation to the truth. Scientific knowledge is not absolute but "optimal"; it contains the optimum of truth attainable in a given historical period. Various cultures have emphasized various aspects of the truth, and the more mankind becomes united culturally, the more will these various aspects become integrated into a total picture.

There is another sense in which ethical norms are not absolute: not only are they subject to revision like all scientific statements, but there are certain situations which are inherently insoluble and do not permit any choice which can be considered "the" right one. Spencer, in his discussion of relative versus absolute ethics,[73] gives an illustration of such a conflict. He speaks of a tenant farmer who wishes to vote in a general election. He knows that his landlord is a conservative and that he risks the chance of eviction if he votes according to his own conviction, which is liberal. Spencer believes that the conflict is one between injuring the state and injuring his family, and he arrives at the result that here as "in countless cases no one can decide by which of the alternative courses the least wrong is likely to be done."[74] The alternative in this case seems not to be correctly stated by Spencer. There would be an ethical conflict even if there were no family involved but only the risk of his own happiness and safety. On the other hand, not only the interest of the state is at stake but also his own integrity. What he is really confronted with is the choice between his physical and thereby also (in some respects) his mental well-being on the one side, and his integrity on the other. Whatever he does

[73] *Principles of Ethics*, pp. 258 ff.
[74] *Ibid.*, p. 267.

is right and wrong at the same time. He can not make a choice which is valid because the problem he faces is inherently insoluble. Such situations of insoluble ethical conflict arise necessarily in connection with existential dichotomies. In this case, however, we deal not with an existential dichotomy which is inherent in the human situation but with a historical dichotomy which can be removed. The tenant farmer is faced with such an unanswerable conflict only because the social order presents him with a situation in which no satisfactory solution is possible. If the social constellation changes, the ethical conflict will disappear. But as long as these conditions exist, any decision he makes is both right and wrong, although the decision in favor of his integrity may be held to be morally superior to that in favor of his life.

The last and the most important meaning in which the terms "absolute" and "relative" ethics are used is one which is more adequately expressed as the difference between *universal* and *socially immanent* ethics. By "universal" ethics I mean norms of conduct the aim of which is the growth and unfolding of man; by "socially immanent" ethics I mean such norms as are necessary for the functioning and survival of a specific kind of society and of the people living in it. An example of the concept of universal ethics may be found in such norms as "Love thy neighbor as thyself" or "Thou shalt not kill." Indeed, the ethical systems of all great cultures show an amazing similarity in what is considered necessary for the development of man, of norms which follow from the nature of man and the conditions necessary for his growth.

By "socially immanent" ethics I refer to those norms in any culture which contain prohibitions and commands that are necessary only for the functioning and survival of that particular society. It is necessary for the survival of any society that its members submit to the rules which are essential to its particular mode of production and mode of life. The group must tend to mold the character structure of its members in such a way that *they want to do what they have to do under* the existing circumstances. Thus, for instance, courage and initiative become imperative virtues for a warrior society, patience and helpfulness become virtues for a society in which agricultural cooperation is dominant. In modern society, industry has been elevated to the position of one of the highest virtues because the modern industrial system needed the drive to work as one of its most important productive forces. The qualities which rank highly in the operation of a particular society become part of its ethical system. Any society has a vital interest in having its rules obeyed and its "virtues" adhered to because its survival depends on this adherence.

In addition to norms in the interest of society as a whole, we find other ethical norms which differ from class to class. A case in point is the emphasis on the virtues of modesty and obedience for the lower classes and of ambition and aggressiveness for the upper classes. The more fixed and institutionalized the class structure is, the more will different sets of norms be explicitly related to different classes, as, for instance, norms for free men or for serfs in a feudal culture, or for whites and Negroes in the southern United States. In modern democratic societies where class differences are not part of the institutionalized structure of society, the different sets of norms are taught side by side: for instance, the ethics of the New Testament and the norms that are effective for the conduct of a successful business. According to one's social position and talent each individual will choose that set of norms which he can use while perhaps continuing to pay lip service to the opposite set. Difference in education at home and in school (as, for instance, in the public schools of England and certain private schools in the United States) tends to emphasize the particular set of values that fits in with the upper-class social position without directly negating the other.

The function of the ethical system in any given society is to sustain the life of that particular society. But such socially immanent ethics is also in the interest of the individual; since the society is structured in a certain way, which he as an individual cannot change, his individual self-interest is bound up with the society's. At the same time the society, however, may be organized in such a way that the norms necessary for its survival conflict with the universal norms necessary for the fullest development of its members. This is especially true in societies in which privileged groups dominate or exploit the rest of the members. The interests of the privileged group conflict with those of the majority, but inasmuch as the society functions on the basis of such a class structure, the norms imposed upon all by the members of the privileged group are necessary for the survival of everybody as long as the structure of the society is not fundamentally changed.

The ideologies prevalent in such a culture will tend to deny that there is any contradiction. They will claim, in the first place, that the ethical norms of that society are of equal value to all its members and will tend to emphasize that those norms which tend to uphold the existing social structure are universal norms resulting from the necessities of human existence. The prohibition against theft, for instance, is often made to appear as springing from the same "human" necessity as does the prohibition against murder. Thus norms which are necessary only in the interest of the survival of a special kind of society are given the dignity of universal norms inherent in human existence and therefore universally applicable. As long as a certain type of social organization is historically indispensable, the individual has no choice but to accept the ethical norms as binding. But when a society retains a structure which operates against the interests of a majority, while the basis for a change is present, the awareness of the socially conditioned character of its norms will become an important element in furthering tendencies to change the social order. Such attempts are usually called unethical by the representatives of the old order. One calls those who want happiness for themselves "selfish" and those who want to retain their privileges, "responsible." Submission, on the other hand, is glorified as the virtue of "unselfishness" and "devotion."

While the conflict between socially immanent and universal ethics has decreased in the process of human evolution, there remains a conflict between the two types of ethics as long as humanity has not succeeded in building a society in which the interest of "society" has become identical with that of all its members. As long as this point has not been reached in human evolution, the historically conditioned social necessities clash with the universal existential necessities of the individual. If the individual lived five hundred or one thousand years, this clash might not exist or at least might be considerably reduced. He then might live and harvest with joy what he sowed in sorrow; the suffering of one historical period which will bear fruit in the next one could bear fruit for him too. But man lives sixty or seventy years and he may never live to see the harvest. Yet he is born as a unique being, having in himself all the potentialities which it is the task of mankind to realize. It is the obligation of the student of the science of man not to seek for "harmonious" solutions, glossing over this contradiction, but to see it sharply. It is the task of the ethical thinker to sustain and strengthen the voice of human conscience, to recognize what is good or what is bad for *man*, regardless of whether it is good or bad for society at a special period of its evolution. He may be the one who "crieth in the wilderness," but only if this voice remains alive and uncompromising will the wilderness change into fertile land. The contradiction between immanent social ethics and universal ethics will be reduced and tend to disappear to the same extent to which society becomes truly human, that is, takes care of the full human development of all its members.

CHAPTER V

THE MORAL PROBLEM OF TODAY

Until philosophers are kings, or the kings and princes of this world have the spirit and power of philosophy, and political greatness and wisdom meet in one, and those commoner natures who pursue either to the exclusion of the other are compelled to stand aside, cities will never have rest from their evils, no, nor the human race, as I believe—and then only will this our State have a possibility of life and behold the light of day.

—Plato, *The Republic*

Is there a special moral problem of *today?* Is not the moral problem one and the same for all times and for all men? Indeed it is, and yet every culture has specific moral problems which grow out of its particular structure, although these specific problems are only various facets of the moral problems of *man.* Any such particular facet can be understood only in relation to the basic and general problem of man. In this concluding chapter I want to emphasize one specific aspect of the general moral problem, partly because it is a crucial one from the psychological viewpoint and partly because we are tempted to evade it, being under the illusion of having solved this very problem: *man's attitude toward force and power.*

Man's attitude toward force is rooted in the

very conditions of his existence. As physical
beings we are subject to power—to the power of
nature and to the power of man. Physical force
can deprive us of our freedom and kill us. Whether
we can resist or overcome it depends on the accidental factors of our own physical strength and
the strength of our weapons. Our mind, on the
other hand, is not directly subject to power. The
truth which we have recognized, the ideas in
which we have faith, do not become invalidated
by force. Might and reason exist on different
planes, and force never disproves truth.

Does this mean that man is free even if he is
born in chains? Does it mean that the spirit of a
slave can be as free as that of his master, as
St. Paul and Luther have maintained? It would
indeed simplify the problem of human existence
tremendously if this were true. But this position
ignores the fact that ideas and the truth do not
exist outside and independently of man, and that
man's mind is influenced by his body, his mental
state by his physical and social existence. Man is
capable of knowing the truth and he is capable of
loving, but if he—not just his body, but he in
his totality—is threatened by superior force, if he
is made helpless and afraid, his mind is affected,
its operations become distorted and paralyzed.
The paralyzing effect of power does not rest only
upon the fear it arouses, but equally on an implicit
promise—the promise that those in possession of
power can protect and take care of the "weak"
who submit to it, that they can free man from the
burden of uncertainty and of responsibility for
himself by guaranteeing order and by assigning
the individual a place in this order which makes
him feel secure.

Man's submission to this combination of threat
and promise is his real "fall." By submitting to
power = domination he loses *his* power = potency. He loses his power to make use of all those

capacities which make him truly human; his
reason ceases to operate; he may be intelligent,
he may be capable of manipulating things and
himself, but he accepts as truth that which those
who have power over him call the truth. He loses
his power of love, for his emotions are tied to
those upon whom he depends. He loses his moral
sense, for his inability to question and criticize
those in power stultifies his moral judgment with
regard to anybody and anything. He is prey to
prejudice and superstition for he is incapable of
inquiring into the validity of the premises upon
which rest such false beliefs. His own voice cannot call him back to himself since he is not able
to listen to it, being so intent on listening to the
voices of those who have power over him. Indeed,
freedom is the necessary condition of happiness as
well as of virtue; freedom, not in the sense of the
ability to make arbitrary choices and not freedom
from necessity, but freedom to realize that which
one potentially is, to fulfill the true nature of man
according to the laws of his existence.

If freedom, the ability to preserve one's integrity against power, is the basic condition for
morality, has man in the Western world not solved
his moral problem? Is it not only a problem of
people living under authoritarian dictatorships
which deprive them of their personal and political
freedom? Indeed, the freedom attained in modern
democracy implies a promise for the development
of man which is absent in any kind of dictator-
ship, regardless of their proclamations that they
act in man's interest. But it is a promise only, and
not yet a fulfillment. We mask our own moral
problem from ourselves if we focus our attention
on comparing our culture with modes of life which
are the negation of the best achievements of
humanity, and thus we ignore the fact that we too
bow down to power, not to that of a dictator and
a political bureaucracy allied with him, but to the

anonymous power of the market, of success, of public opinion, of "common sense"—or rather, of common nonsense—and of the machine whose servants we have become.

Our moral problem is man's indifference to himself. It lies in the fact that we have lost the sense of the significance and uniqueness of the individual, that we have made ourselves into instruments for purposes outside ourselves, that we experience and treat ourselves as commodities, and that our own powers have become alienated from ourselves. We have become things and our neighbors have become things. The result is that we feel powerless and despise ourselves for our impotence. Since we do not trust our own power, we have no faith in man, no faith in ourselves or in what our own powers can create. We have no conscience in the humanistic sense, since we do not dare to trust our judgment. We are a herd believing that the road we follow must lead to a goal since we see everybody else on the same road. We are in the dark and keep up our courage because we hear everybody else whistle as we do.

Dostoyevsky once said, "If God is dead, everything is allowed." This is, indeed, what most people believe; they differ only in that some draw the conclusion that God and the church must remain alive in order to uphold the moral order, while others accept the idea that everything is allowed, that there is no valid moral principle, that expediency is the only regulative principle in life.

In contrast, humanistic ethics takes the position that *if man is alive he knows what is allowed;* and to be alive means to be productive, to use one's powers not for any purpose transcending man, but for oneself, to make sense of one's existence, to be human. As long as anyone believes that his ideal and purpose is outside him, that it is above the clouds, in the past or in the future, he will go outside himself and seek fulfillment where it can not be found. He will look for solutions and answers at every point except the one where they can be found—in himself.

The "realists" assure us that the problem of ethics is a relic of the past. They tell us that psychological or sociological analysis shows that all values are only relative to a given culture. They propose that our personal and social future is guaranteed by our material effectiveness alone. But these "realists" are ignorant of some hard facts. They do not see that the emptiness and planlessness of individual life, that the lack of productiveness and the consequent lack of faith in oneself and in mankind, if prolonged, result in emotional and mental disturbances which would incapacitate man even for the achievement of his material aims.

Prophecies of doom are heard today with increasing frequency. While they have the important function of drawing attention to the dangerous possibilities in our present situation they fail to take into account the promise which is implied in man's achievement in the natural sciences, in psychology, in medicine and in art. Indeed, these achievements portray the presence of strong productive forces which are not compatible with the picture of a decaying culture. Our period is a period of transition. The Middle Ages did not end in the fifteenth century, and the modern era did not begin immediately afterward. End and beginning imply a process which has lasted over four hundred years—a very short time indeed if we measure it in historical terms and not in terms of our life span. Our period is an end and a beginning, pregnant with possibilities.

If I repeat now the question raised in the beginning of this book, whether we have reason to be proud and to be hopeful, the answer is again in the affirmative, but with the one qualification which follows from what we have discussed throughout: neither the good nor the evil outcome is automatic or preordained. The decision rests with man. It rests upon his ability to take himself, his life and happiness seriously; on his willingness to face his and his society's moral problem. It rests upon his courage to be himself and to be for himself.

INDEX

Activity, 26, 27, 34, 74–75, 91–94, 98–99, 112, 178, 179, 180, 193, 196, 198, 210, 231, 232
Adler, Mortimer J., 40
Aquinas, Thomas, 213
Approval-disapproval, 167
Aristippus, 177
Aristotle, concept of activity, 92, 98; on art, 27, 34, 39; on love, 128; on the science of man, 34–35; in relation to pleasure and happiness, 179, 182; on productiveness, 98
Art, 26–28, 106, 192, 209, 250
Assimilation, 66, 67 et seq.
Augustine. St., 154, 213, 214
Authoritarian character, 93, 148–62, 169–70, 214, 223. See also Exploitative character
Authoritarian ethics, see Ethical norms
Authority, 15, 18–22, 24–25, 93, 148–62, 170, 171, 172, 174, 175, 176, 204, 205, 206, 207, 208

Bally, G., 189
Balzac, 64, 114
Behavior patterns (traits), 31, 62–64, 65, 67
Bergson, H., 94
Brentano, 94
Buddha, 44, 109
Butler, 147

Calvin, 124–26, 127, 139, 154, 214, 223
Character, 155, 200, 216, 217, 227, 242; and behavior, 41–

42, 62–64, 65, 67; dynamic concept of, 62 et seq.; in relation to human nature; 47 et seq.; the neurotic, 25, 32, 41, 90; and personality, 17; and genital sexuality, 90; its relation to virtue, 45; and moral judgment, 232–38. See also Exploitative, Hoarding, Market, Loving and Receptive character types
Chrysippus, 147
Cicero, 147
Conscience, 145–48, 234; authoritarian, 148–62; humanistic, 162–75

Destructiveness, 155, 213, 215–16, 217–18, 227–30, 236
Dewey, John, 34, 41; ethics and psychology, 39; means-ends relationships, 37–38; value judgments and inquiry, 37
Dichotomy, 48–54, 221, 241
Dilthey, 94
Dostoyevsky, 249
Doubt, 202

Education, 83, 160, 209, 211
Engels, 130
Epicurus, 25, 178
Equality, 81
Ethical norms, 123 et seq.; absolute vs. relativistic. 238–45; authoritarian, 18–24, 30; and human nature, 16; humanistic, 18, 21–23, 27–29, 34–39; and moral powers in man, 212 et seq.; and the moral

253